SALT W

ANDREW MOTION

Salt Water

FABER & FABER

First published in 1997
by Faber & Faber Ltd
Bloomsbury House
74–77 Great Russell Street
London WC1B 3DA
This paperback edition first published in 2019

Photoset by Wilmaset Ltd, Wirral
Printed in the UK by TJ International Ltd, Padstow, Cornwall

A CIP record for this book is available from the British Library

ISBN 978–0–571–35601–0

FSC
www.fsc.org
MIX
Paper from
responsible sources
FSC® C013056

10 9 8 7 6 5 4 3 2 1

For Jan
and Jesse, Sidonie and Lucas

We were not many minutes on the road, though we sometimes stopped to lay hold of each other and hearken. But there was no unusual sound – nothing but the low wash of the ripple and the croaking of the crows in the wood.

Robert Louis Stevenson, *Treasure Island*

Acknowledgements

Acknowledgements are due to the following: BBC Radio 4; BBC World Service; the *Guardian*; the *Independent on Sunday*; the *London Review of Books*; the *Poetry Quarterly*; *Sibila* (Seville); the *Times Literary Supplement*.

'Dead March' first appeared in *On the Death of a Parent*, edited by Jane McLoughlin (Virago, 1994), and 'Reading the Elephant' in *A Parcel of Poems* (Faber, 1995).

'Does That Hurt?' was first published in a limited edition by Prospero Poets (1995), with illustrations by Rigby Graham.

Contents

PART ONE

Fresh Water

In Memory of Ruth Haddon

1

This is a long time ago. I am visiting my brother, who is living
near Cirencester, and he says let's go and see the source of the
                                                          Thames.
It's winter. We leave early, before the sun has taken frost off the
                                                          fields,

and park in a lane. There's a painful hawthorn hedge with a
                                                          stile.
When we jump down, our boots gibber on the hard ground.
Then we're striding, kicking ice-dust off the grass to look
                                                  confident –

because really we're not sure if we're allowed to be here.
In fact we're not even sure that this is the right place.
A friend of a friend has told us; it's all as vague as that.

In the centre of the field we find more hawthorn, a single
                                                          bush,
and water oozing out of a hole in the ground. I tell my brother
I've read about a statue that stands here, or rather lounges
                                                  here –

a naked, shaggy-haired god tilting an urn with one massive
                                                          hand.
Where is he? There's only the empty field glittering,
and a few dowager cows picking among the dock-clumps.

Where is Father Thames? My brother thinks he has been
                                                      vandalised
and dragged off by the fans of other rivers – they smashed the
                                                      old man's urn,
and sprayed his bare chest and legs with the names of rivals:

Trent, Severn, Nene, Humber. There's nothing else to do,
so I paddle through the shallow water surrounding the spring,
treading carefully to keep things in focus,

and stoop over the source as though I find it fascinating.
It is fascinating. A red-brown soft-lipped cleft
with bright green glass right up to the edge,

and the water twisting out like a rope of glass.
It pulses and shivers as it comes, then steadies
into the pool, then roughens again as it drains into the valley.

My brother and I are not twenty yet. We don't know who we
                                                      are,
or who we want to be. We stare at the spring, at each other,
and back at the spring again, saying nothing.

A pheasant is making its blatant *kok-kok*
from the wood running along the valley floor.
I stamp both feet and disappear in a cloud.

2

One March there's suddenly a day as warm as May, and my
                                                      friend
uncovers the punt he has bought as a wreck and restored,
cleans her, slides her into the Thames near Lechlade, and sets off

upriver. Will I go with him? No, I can't.
But I'll meet him on the water meadows at the edge of town.
I turn out of the market square, past the church, and down
                                    the yew-tree walk.

Shelley visited here once – it's called Shelley's Walk –
but he was out of his element. Here everything is earth
and water, not fire and air. The ground is sleepy-haired

after winter, red berries and rain matted into it.
Where the yew-tree walk ends I go blind in the sun for a
                                    moment,
then it's all right. There's the river beyond the boggy meadows,

hidden by reed-forests sprouting along its banks. They're
                                    dead,
the reeds – a shambles of broken, broad, pale-brown leaves
and snapped bullrush heads. And there's my friend making

his slow curve towards me. The hills rise behind him
in a gradual wave, so that he seems at the centre
of an enormous amphitheatre. He is an emblem of something;

somebody acting something. The punt pole shoots up
wagging its beard of light, falls, and as he moves ahead
he leans forward, red-faced and concentrating.

He's expert but it's slow work. As I get closer I can hear
water pattering against the prow of the punt,
see him twisting the pole as he plucks it out of the gluey
                                    river-bed.

I call to him and he stands straight, giving a wobbly wave.
We burst into laughter. He looks like a madman, floating
                                                  slowly
backwards now that he has stopped poling. I must look

like a madman too, mud-spattered and heavy-footed on the
                                                  bank,
wondering how I'm going to get on board without falling in.
As I push open the curtain of leaves to find a way,

I see the water for the first time, solid-seeming and mercury-
                                                  coloured.
Not like a familiar thing at all. Not looking
as though it could take us anywhere we wanted to go.

3

I've lived here for a while, and up to now the river has been
for pleasure. This evening people in diving suits have taken it
                                                  over.
Everyone else has been shooshed away into Christchurch
                                                  Meadow

or onto Folly Bridge like me. No one's complaining. The
                                        summer evening
expands lazily, big purple and gold clouds building over the
                                        Cumnor hills.
I have often stood here before. Away to the left you can see
                                                  Oxford

throwing its spires into the air, full of the conceited joy of
                                                    being itself.
Straight ahead the river runs calmly between boat-houses
before losing patience again, pulling a reed-shawl round its ears,

snapping off willows and holding their scarified heads
                                                    underwater.
Now there's a small rowing boat, a kind of coracle below me,
and two policemen with their jackets off. The men shield their
                                                    eyes,

peering, and almost rock overboard, they're so surprised,
when bubbles erupt beside them and a diver bobs up –
just his head, streaming in its black wet-suit. There are shouts –

See anything? – but the diver shrugs, and twirls his murky
                                                    torchlight
with an invisible hand. Everyone on the bridge stops talking.
We think we are about to be shown the story of the river-bed –

its shopping trolleys and broken boat-parts, its lolling bottles,
its plastic, its dropped keys, its blubbery and bloated corpse.
But nothing happens. The diver taps his mask and disappears,

his fart-trail surging raucously for a moment, then subsiding.
The crowd in Christchurch Meadow starts to break up.
On Folly Bridge people begin talking again, and as someone
                                                    steps

off the pavement onto the road, a passing grocery van –
irritated by the press of people, and impatient with whatever
brought them together – gives a long wild *paarp* as it revs
                                                    away.

[7]

4

Now the children are old enough to see what there is to see
we take them to Tower Bridge and explain how the road lifts up,
how traitors arrived at Traitor's Gate, how this was a brewery

and that was a warehouse, how the river starts many miles
                                                    inland
and changes and grows, changes and grows, until it arrives here,
London, where we live, then winds past Canary Wharf

(which they've done in school) and out to sea.
Afterwards we lean on the railings outside a café. It's autumn.
The water is speckled with leaves, and a complicated tangle of
                                                    junk

bumps against the embankment wall: a hank of bright grass,
a rotten bullrush stem, a fragment of dark polished wood.
One of the children asks if people drown in the river, and I
                                                    think

of Ruth, who was on the *Marchioness*. After her death, I met
someone who had survived. He had been in the lavatory when
                                        the dredger hit,
and fumbled his way out along a flooded corridor, his shoes

and clothes miraculously slipping off him, so that when he at
                                                    last
burst into the air he felt that he was a baby again
and knew nothing, was unable to help himself, aghast.

I touch my wife's arm and the children gather round us.
We are the picture of a family on an outing. I love it. I love the
river
and the perky tour-boats with their banal chat. I love the snub
barges.

I love the whole dazzling cross-hatchery of traffic and currents,
shadows and sun, standing still and moving forward.
The tangle of junk bumps the wall below me again and I look
down.

There is Ruth swimming back upstream, her red velvet party
dress
flickering round her heels as she twists through the locks
and dreams round the slow curves, slithering on for miles

until she has passed the ponderous diver at Folly Bridge
and the reed-forests at Lechlade, accelerating beneath bridges
and willow branches,
slinking easily among the plastic wrecks and weedy trolleys,

speeding and shrinking and silvering until finally she is sliding
uphill
over bright green grass and into the small wet mouth of the
earth,
where she vanishes.

Reading the Elephant

For Ted Hughes

I won't say much about it now, except that she got
bored, or I did, at any rate someone left someone,
there was a leaving, and quite by chance
I had this friend of a friend who said why not
run away for a bit, it won't seem like running,
it won't when you say it's to Africa, God no,
that sounds like choice. So I did. I went like a shot.

And the next thing I knew was this place
marooned in the trees – that is: in the hills,
except it was trees I could see, no two the same
and swarming right up to the house – one with a face
in its trunk like a skinny-jawed Rackham witch,
one a cedar of some sort though really like clouds,
slabs of green cloud which boiled straight up into space.

It had people there too, of course, but they left me
as well, or rather I chose to stay put. Come morning
they'd clatter out into the jeep with their hampers,
their cameras, their hip-flasks, and set off to see
whatever strayed into their paths (one day a lion
shagged out on a comfortable branch, the next a croc
rip-roaring a bambi, just like they do on TV).

I'd walk round in circles indoors and wait until no one
was looking – in circles, but never unhappy, just
turning time back on itself. You know how it is.
Then I'd slither away to a spot where the sun
splayed down through those trees I was talking about

like a bicycle tyre, and set myself square to the world
as though everything in it had only that moment begun.

I mean: as though never till then had the daylight
come razoring over that silver-grey scrub,
never till then had the dust of that infinite landscape
been glued into cones of such a miraculous height
by ants with such staggering brains, never till then
had leaves been shelter or simply the things that they were –
pure pattern, pure beauty, pure pleasure in living, pure sight.

They never last long, these moments. With half a chance
we drop back to life as it is. I understand that.
I'm not quite a fool. So to keep myself airborne I always
snapped open some book (some parachute) just as my trance
was ending – which meant on the day that I'm thinking about
I'd turned to Pierre and was hearing how Moscow must fall
this month, what with the winter, what with the French
                                              advance.

Soldiers fanned out on the steppes. Feathers of smoke
flapped above burnt-out farms. An immense chandelier
reflected bare shoulders and medals revolving in miniature,
time and again, as the string quartet for a joke
performed by a wide-open window for Boney to hear,
each note struck fierce and hard and long on the dark
like stones sent skittering out on a windless lake –

like something inside me, yet outside as well,
a fracture, a cracking, which made me whisk round,
heart jumping, and find there not ten yards behind,
stock still in the African day I could no longer tell
was real – an elephant. Elephant.

Huge as a hill, creased where the weather runs down,
grave-grey in the haze of its dry-grass-pissed-on smell

and staring me out. That lasted I don't know how long –
the eyes not blinking no matter how busily flies
kept fussing and dabbling, the ragged-edged ears
traced with lugubrious veins, the bristly thong
of its tail twitched side to side, and me just sitting
not thinking at all – at least, me thinking that never
would one of the several worlds I was living among

connect with another, that soon I would just disappear
as the elephant would, its baggy-skinned legs
slow-pumping, its tentative feet squashing down
on their silent compressors, and leaving the air
disturbed for only a moment, no more, as I did myself
when I saw that enough was enough, and escaped
from the trees into unbroken sunlight with everything clear.

The Spoilt Child

It was a privilege to ride out
from the stables with his mother:
the world belonged to them,
they belonged to each other

and the labrador puppy slinking
beside them in and out of the hedge—
she belonged to them too;
she was part of the privilege,

trotting to heel just like that
as soon as the order came,
so all three seemed like mechanical toys
whose journey was always the same,

always began in the deep blackberry lane
softly, hooves cushioned on gravel,
then unwound gradually into the village
where mother and son appeared at window-level

trying hard not to stare in
through veils of variously figured lace
at lives they were happy to see lived
as long as each knew its place.

Here they never quite came to a halt,
only pretended they might be slowing
down sometimes for *Thank you; thank you—
and now, really, we must be going,*

before clopping on towards open country,
their minds filled with nothing—
or rather, filled with the thought
of lush meadows, hooves thundering,

and every horizon they might choose to face
splitting open like water in front of a prow,
or splitting like earth itself
under the keel of a plough,

and going on splitting until—
as if it were dust striking his eye—
the boy saw a dog, a bull terrier,
apparently drop from the sky

and flatten the beautiful labrador puppy
still trotting neatly at his side,
roll her so she was pale belly side up,
plant his bow legs astride,

and latch onto her neck. What comfort
then was his mother, shutting her eyes?
She might give her little scream,
she might cry,

but the outrageous teeth stayed locked
in the sleek golden throat,
and when the boy at last dismounted to look
they were bright shining wet

with the brilliant life-blood of his pet,
making him feel he was no use at all

no matter how he might thwack his whip
on the bull terrier's head, and call

for his beloved to rise up and fight,
and go on using his whip again, then again
and again, until at last giving way
when a stranger butted in—

a beery man wearing a vest,
and undone, down-trodden shoes,
who carried an all-metal hammer
and a stone he intended to drive through

the bull terrier's teeth to shatter them
if there was no chance of prising them loose,
which he decided at once there wasn't,
giving one, two, three steady blows,

with the pop-eyed boy watching
and the mother now covering her face,
before sinking down onto his knees:
Jesus; Jesus. Right then – in that case –

and finally hammering the stone
so far in, it stuck out the other side
of the terrier's foaming mouth,
opening it up wide

and leaving the puppy's neck plain
for the boy to see:
the pink windpipe, the oyster-coloured muscles
like a lesson in biology.

Sorry, I'm sorry, the mother and son
then thought they would hear the man say.
What they got was a single deep grunt
and a slow turn away –

It's all right, he said. *I'll deal with her now.*
It's all right. It's all right. Ah, but you see
they thought he was lying. Nothing was right
any more, nothing could change history –

and now, if nobody minded . . . ?
They set off home at the trot, and never looked round
once at the stranger watching them go, his dog in pain,
their own splayed on the ground.

A Severe Absence of Fish

Even the most masterful of Zen Grand Masters
might lose patience and want time to run faster

if, waist-deep like me in this bitterly cold river
all week, he had cast his truest cast over and over –

casting with all the passionate concentration of will
a person can possibly have when they are trying to kill

something they love, and leaving no secret lie
untouched by the slick, expressionless, heartless fly,

no lee of a dark rock, no pool, no plausible run,
no mysterious shadow, no patch of sleepy sun –

which means (remember: I'm casting over and over)
all day my head is my own, intent on the river,

and also clean off my shoulders, full of whatever else
might come along next: the wall-eyed head of a grilse

an otter chewed off and left on its feasting stone
bleakly to catch the light; then the otter alone

and playing, in and out of the water so fast, so deft
I am always agog at the place it has suddenly left;

then one silly Canada goose flying miles above my head,
the creak of its wing-beat like you turning over in bed.

Yes, that's right. What comes along next. One thing
just slithering after another like beads down a string

and away into nothing, the nothing that day after day
I carefully enter and wade through, finding a way

to bring its cold surface to life, to fill empty space
with a rising, drawn, dead-pan, strenuous face reflecting my
                                                    face.

Dead March

It's twenty years (*It's not, it's twenty-three –*
be accurate) since you were whisked away
(*I wasn't 'whisked away': I broke my skull*)
and I was left to contemplate your life.
(*My life? Ridiculous. You mean my death.*)

Well, twenty/twenty-three. I can't decide
if that's a long time or no time at all,
or whether everything I've said since then,
and thought and done, to try and work out how
the way we treat our lives might be involved
with how our lives treat us is more than just
a waste of breath. That's right. A waste of breath.

You see, you're always with me even though
you're nowhere, nothing, dead to all the world –
you interrupt me when I start to talk,
you are the shadow dragging at my heels.
This means I can't step far enough away
to get the thing I want you to explain
in focus, and I can't lean close enough
to hear the words you speak and feel their weight.

And if I could, what difference would it make?
It's like I said. I can't decide. It's just
that having you suspended all these years
at some clear mid-point between life and death
has made me think you might have felt your way

along the link between the two, and learnt
how one deserves the other. Or does not.

I feel I'm standing on a frozen pond
entranced by someone else below the ice,
a someone who has found out how to breathe
the water and endure the cold and dark.
I know I ought to turn my back. I can't.
I also know that if I just stay put
and watch the wax-white fingers flop about
I'll start to think they must be beckoning.
I stare and stare and stare and stare and stare.
It's twenty years since you were whisked away,
or twenty-three. That's more than half my life.

Does That Hurt?

With grass on the quarry floor knee-high;
with invisible larks showering down song
from the far side of the sky;

with oak-scrub and bramble the only shade;
with ants in their deep forest keeping track
of every journey they've made;

with glittering flint-hills gradually bleeding sand;
with the body of one rusting mechanical digger
stooped over its snapped-off hand;

with my small son steadily smaller at my side;
with what we have left of the quarry to cross
stretching too wide, too wide;

with a dog-rose barrier guarding the high ledge ahead;
with hearts hobbling when finally we flop there
shot-down-dead;

with a fat stinging bee dropping out of a flower well-fed;
with the same bee losing its grip on the air and stumbling
onto my son's head;

with screaming and panic which swipes the poison in;
with my pantomime brushing and flapping *keep still!*
achieving nothing;

with the entire horizon a tight circle of pain;
with the flint-hills, the long-drawn-out quarry floor
hateful to think of again;

with larks still rising out of the world in their crazy trance;
with the earth itself crying the cry
of mere existence.

*

It's not just him I see,
not just his soft weight
I lift and bring with me,

no, not just him, it's you,
your weight as well,
your pain brand-new

however long it lasts,
which now means years,
means each day still your first

at sea, unwillingly afloat,
your big high-pillowed bed
a raft which marks the site

where everything you knew
went down, and you the one
survivor spared to show

the way pain looks, and loss,
and life alone,
and grief without redress:

its sticky breath,
its tongue which cannot budge and longs
to ask for death.

*

Does that hurt? Don't be a fool.
My finger-end blunders about
to close the wild eye of his sting.

Does that hurt? Don't be a fool.
It hurts as much as he knows,
but I tell him he's sure to live.

Does that hurt? Don't be a fool.
He flinches away with the pain
already a story: remember that bee?

Does that hurt? Don't be a fool.
He's off while the day we began with
still has some time left to run.

Does that hurt? Don't be a fool.
Just look at me watching him go
and you'd say I felt nothing at all.

Your Postcard Came

Your postcard came: a snap of Mediterranean blue
and bright chatter ending: How are you?

How am *I*? How are *you* is what I want to know –
last month checked over, stitched up, blasted with chemo

and now adrift, floating through days of slow sun
with one part of life finished, the next not yet begun.

And something else. I want to know too why the hell
last time you came to visit me at home I couldn't tell

how much better I might have made you feel
(no, 'loved', not 'better'; 'better' is too genteel)

if, instead of slipping out into the garden quietly
to pick the apples from our wet-leaved, sagging tree

– you said you felt like sleeping – I had just stayed close
and kept you talking. What came over me? Do I suppose

we'll always have enough time left for that?
That's shit.

The second I had propped
my ladder gingerly against the tree and crept

within its brittle globe – *hold tight! a child again!* –
and started rattling down the apple-rain,

I looked back at the house and found your face
inside the window like a silhouette in ice

and melting – skin becoming water and then air
before I stretched to pull the apples near,

the apples swelling air and water in their new-made skin.
How am I? I shall tell you, then.

I'm wishing you were here and well, that's all.
Not thinking how I climbed while you were waiting for the
fall.

In Memory of Zoë Yalland

First this: your boxed-in, low-browed, hunched-up mews,
you quinced by your divorce, no space, no sun,
the market barrows waking you at five,
and dog shit, midnight blarings, nothing done
to make you feel the house might be your home,
but you still battling, hoping luck could run
right out and still come back, insisting life
of any kind was preferable to none,
and thinking (more like praying) that with time
just staying still meant starting to belong.

Then this: your slack-stringed hand which cannot lift
is grey with cancer, bones all eaten through,
and crumples on your pillow with the sleeve
of that stiff nightdress they have given you
dragged down and open by its own crisp weight
to give a glimpse – no, no, a whole long view
along the inside of your arm, your skin
such parchment, such unblemished white-and-blue,
it seems you're living backwards, seems you might
be young again, and well, and free to live. Not true.

The Clearing

Further than I usually go,
where the river path winds through
pine-ranks with bayonets fixed,
heather-ramparts which have me banjaxed,
rowan-redoubts, thorn-barricades, warren-pits
and long minefields of silver bog and moss,
I drop without warning down into nowhere,
into a tight clearing of unbreathed air,
and feel nothing at first – just light
collecting and losing its feeble heat,
just mosquitoes dotting my face and hands
with their mad rush of stinging sand–
and see nothing either, not even the river
which smoothes one side of the little theatre,
not the pines or marshes which cut me off
from the world I have now completely left,
only a tree-trunk raised to the empty sky,
a trunk stripped bare, twenty feet high,
and topped with what I suppose is a face –
the hair a wig of marram grass,
the skull a basket of dry sticks,
the eyes bright stone, the mouth a block
of something like balsa or black cork
and fissured with thousands of tiny cracks,
so that no matter how sunlight spills,
no matter what softening shadows fall,
it has one set expression and one
alone: a look of suffering begun
so long ago and felt so utterly

no sense remains of how the world could be
without it, how an eye could shine
with something other than the pain
of just enduring, simply going on,
or how a mind could think the someone
who created it (who built it God
knows how and God knows when) had
hoped they might be making something else –
a joke, a thing so clearly false
in all its famished misery and hurt
that anyone who found it might
just laugh, might simply clamber back
along the barricaded river track
into their normal lives again and think
that nothing anywhere deserves a look
as bleak and beaten-out as this face shows.
Who knows, I ask myself. Who knows?

Goethe in the Park

The slates have gone
from that shed in the park
where sometimes the old sat
if they were desperate,
and sometimes the young
with nowhere better to fuck,

and now given some luck
the whole piss-stinking thing
will fall to the ground,
no, I mean
will lift into space,
no evidence left

in its earthly place
of the grey graffiti runes,
the deck of glue,
the bench with broken ribs,
where if things had been different
I might have sat, or you.

This moral won't do.
Think of Goethe who
all those centuries back
found a pure space like that,
his bench an oak tree trunk,
his view

a plain of ripening wheat
where retriever-dog winds
in a clear track
raced forwards and back
laying a new idea at his feet
again and again,

again and again,
but not one the same,
until he was stuffed full
as one of those new-fangled air-balloons
and floated clear
into a different stratosphere.

The oak tree stayed,
its reliable trunk
making light of the sun,
its universe of leaves
returning just as they pleased
each spring, so life begun

was really life carried on,
or was
until a lightning bolt
drove hell-bent
through the iron bark
and split the oak in two.

This moral still won't do.
You see
one crooked piece of tree
broke free,

escaped the fire, and found its way
into the safe hands of a carpenter.

This man, he liked a shed.
(I should explain:
two hundred years have gone
since Goethe saw
the future run towards him
through the wide wheat plain.)

That's right; he liked a shed.
He liked the way a roof
could be a lid
and shut down heavily
to make a box,
a box which locked

so no one saw inside
the ranks
of gimcrack bunks,
or heard things said
by shapes that lay on them
with shaved heads,

not even him.
He just made what was ordered
good and sure,
saw everything was kept
the same, each nail,
each duckboard floor,

except, above one door
in pride of place

he carved his bit of tree,
not thinking twice,
into a face,
a merry gargoyle grimace.

This moral still won't do.
It's after dark,
and on my short-cut home to you
across the park
I smell the shed
before I see it: piss and glue

and something like bad pears,
and yet,
next thing I know
I've stepped inside it,
sat down on the bench
(it isn't pears, it's shit)

and stared up through
its rafters at the stars —
their dead and living lights
which all appear
the same to me,
and settle equally.

To Whom It May Concern

This poem about ice cream
has nothing to do with government,
with riot, with any political scheme.

It is a poem about ice cream. You see?
About how you might stroll into a shop
and ask: *One Strawberry Split. One Mivvi.*

What did I tell you? No one will die.
No licking tongues will melt like candle wax.
This is a poem about ice cream. Do not cry.

Tortoise

Here is a man who served his generals faithfully
and over the years had everything shot away
starting from the feet and working upwards:
feet, legs, chest, arms, neck, head.
In the end he was just a rusting helmet
on the lip of a trench. Then his chin-strap went.

So he became a sort of miraculous stone,
miraculous not just for the fine varnish
which shows every colour right to the depths —
black, topaz, yellow, white, grey, green —
but for the fact it can move. You see?
Four legs and a head and off he goes.

There's only one place to find the future now —
right under his nose — and no question either
where the next meal might be coming from:
jasmine, rose, cactus, marigold, iris, fuschia,
all snow their flowers round him constantly
and all in their different ways are so delicious.

It explains why there is no reason to hurry.
The breeze blows, the blossoms fall, and the head
shambles in and out as the mouth munches:
remorseless, tight, crinkled, silent, toothless, pink.
Life is not difficult any more, oh no; life is simple.
It makes you pause, doesn't it? It makes you think.

Glen Ellen Stories

For Roy & Aisling Foster

You must know already about uncle Ollie
who drove here from England in a JCB.
Think of it jouncing on the ferry.
Think of the tyre-tracks through Killarney.
Now he's the biggest big shot in Kerry
grubbing up boulders and downing trees –
the dinosaur king of the whole county.

And I dare say everything known about Liz
long ago travelled beyond this parish.
How she blazed too bright in her Glory Days.
How her house split open and let in the sky.
Now she is living quite without gravity,
hauling herself each night upstairs
with a rope she somehow slung over a star.

And you'll also have heard about Des and Pat
who found new ways of murdering trout.
A dynamite stick tossed into the lake.
The massive catch of a water-spout.
Now Des is deaf as a sheet of slate
and Pat just sits or ambles about;
he can't figure out where their profits went.

Which in the roundabout way of talk
brings me at last to the Mass Rock.
Real rock, I mean, but also a relic.

The secret altar the English wrecked.
Now where the dead priest did his work
buzz-saws chew up pines for matchsticks.
Go there, will you, and take a look.

Friendly Fire

Candlelight on a raised and gleaming glass –
    once this was friendly fire;
the bright eye of a treat cigar –
    once this was friendly fire;
ghost-shadows vaulting in a deep chimney –
    once this was friendly fire.

A spark waking the plane on its quivering runway –
    then this became friendly fire;
light gilding a wing-tip streaming him south –
    then this became friendly fire;
sunset in a new continent of clouds –
    then this became friendly fire.

Flame-tongues licking him all over in a second –
    now this is friendly fire;
eyes melting into tears too hot to fall –
    now this is friendly fire;
the heart boiled in its own blood –
    now this is friendly fire.

Rain-water glossing a closed circle of roses –
    at last this will be friendly fire;
the pale glare of a coffin tilting into the earth –
    at last this will be friendly fire;
blanks cracked through empty and echoing air –
    at last this will be friendly fire.

Envoy

In the blue bay of green island
unmapped somewhere in the Pacific
a white boat anchors without a design,

that is by chance, and a lone yachtsman
clambers ashore for no reason except to look.
The forest is dense, dense and more hushed

than anywhere seen by the sailor before,
but as he skips up the cindery beach
the trees ahead suddenly shake and there stands

an ancient Japanese soldier, or so he supposes.
(Ancient because his whole body has dried to a nut;
a Japanese soldier because he is still wearing one

thick army boot which is minus the lace to tie it,
and also a tan forage cap with a badge of the sun
set at the low and correct military angle.)

The sailor has never once shouldered arms
but he understands what the soldier thinks:
he thinks the war is still happening somewhere –

the war which has somehow left him behind
or which he escaped – and has not even heard
of the bomb, and what followed after.

But all the same he has suffered enough,
living for twenty-five years and more
on nuts and rain, snake-meat and grass,

and now he is holding aloft to the sailor,
in both his hands, the curved ceremonial sword
he has kept in its brown leather sheath and wonders

please would the sailor like him to break it?
The sailor, who needless to say cannot speak
Japanese and is anyway tongue-tied,

takes the sword, admires it carefully, then
supposes the honourable thing is to hand it back,
which he does, before saying a word or two

to explain how he wants to look over the island,
just quickly, you know, before taking the soldier
with him away from all this and back to the world.

None of which means a thing. The nut-bodied soldier
watches the sailor plunge into the forest and vanish,
re-settles his cap, dredges a faded memory up

of how to sail, swims out to the yacht, and goes.
He believes it is some kind of swap. He feels
his turn has come to try and arrange the peace.

Breaking

I was a child but might have been any age
when this Sunday arrived and time to kill
but how? By talking? By lounging around?
No, all that was dull. By tagging along
with some others who rattled a stick in my gate
to call me out. (Others, you see, not friends.)

We drifted away through the village, its boundary-
field scraped flat for the plan of a new estate
with things like tent-pegs stuck in, with tapes
which held us up for a while as we traipsed
from room to invisible room, invented stairs,
and plumply sat ourselves down on cushions of air.

A mile beyond that was a proper house
(proper meant diamond panes, half-timbered, intact;
proper meant real) but nowhere I'd seen before.
No wonder. It stood so far from the world
it might have been dropped from a plane, or plucked
(I was thinking of books) straight out of the earth on a wish.

Anyway: someone a lifetime ago had thought
the way it tucked in on that narrow plateau
overlooking the valley was perfect: the village
remote but clear (its windows each night
a miniature Milky Way); the woodland beyond
a line of defense which kept every detail in place.

Who says they were wrong? Nothing we found
said anyone living there went to the bad, or worse –
only that time had run out. In boredom perhaps.
More likely (we fingered the eye-height letter-box
open and gazed down the track of the empty hall)
in death, not that we said so aloud.

But it made us feel free to break in –
with somebody smashing a window-pane,
the rest slip-sliding clean through
amazed at ourselves, as if in one step
from the sill to the bare wooden floor we had left
whatever it was we knew and started to dream.

Pale squares on the walls where pictures had hung;
a hand-shaped burn by the grate where a log
once popped; a zig-zag wallpaper rip at the turn
of the stairs where they angled the furniture out;
a slug gone mad in a basin; a giant turd
and no paper blocking the downstairs bog.

Everywhere something beginning its journey
to nothing – or so we imagined, when one of us
(still in our dream) decided that what had been started
slowly should end in a rush, and dragged indoors
from the garden, the hopeless garden, a pole
he said had been cruelly holding a tree to a wall.

There must have been six or so helping,
young, like I say, and every one keen and fit.
We did the walls first – impossibly hard at a glance
but easy as soon as the first crack appeared:

our fingers squirmed in and tore them clean back
to rib-cage wattle and spars, like flensing a corpse.

Then grates (hard work for not much return).
Then windows (but quietly). Then to the bog
to unfetter that agonised turd. Then stairs.
Lastly the floor-boards, working like painters
carefully in from the corners to meet all together
at once by the narrow front door. Then shut it. Then kick it in.

And then spin away down the valley and off
to our homes before it got late. I told you just now,
they were others, these people, not friends,
and even before we came close to the village
I knew I would never be with them again,
not if that's what I chose. It was what I chose.

Dandering in through the sketched-out estate
I fell back and left them without even saying good-bye.
The tent-peg things were still there, and the tapes,
and the stripped-away earth. I just needed some time
to think about what I had done. I had to be sure
this thing I had helped to create would always be mine.

On the Table

I would like to make it clear that I have bought
this tablecloth with its simple repeating pattern
of dark purple blooms not named by any botanist
because it reminds me of that printed dress you had
the summer we met – a dress you have always said
I never told you I liked. Well I did, you know. I did.
I liked it a lot, whether you were inside it or not.

How did it slip so quietly out of our life?
I hate – I really hate – to think of some other bum
swinging those heavy flower-heads left to right.
I hate even more to think of it mouldering on a tip
or torn to shreds – a piece here wiping a dipstick,
a piece there tied round a crack in a lead pipe.

It's all a long time ago now, darling, a long time,
but tonight just like our first night here I am
with my head light in my hands and my glass full,
staring at the big drowsy petals until they start to swim,
loving them but wishing to lift them aside, unbutton them,
tear them, even, if that's what it takes to get through
to the beautiful, moon-white, warm, wanting skin of you.

Hey Nonny

I thought when the glass dropped and did not break
that the world I lived and breathed in was a fake,

and throwing the same glass out through a window
to hear it actually smash on the brick path below

didn't mean: *Oh, that's all right then, everything's OK,*
it meant thinking: *I see. Brilliant. In every possible way*

this fake is complete and perfect. Look at the stem —
a shattered icicle; look at the brim no longer a brim;

look at those two horny dogs which heard the crash
now swivelled apart, heads down and off in a rush.

That shows how complete and perfect. Everything just
a make-believe of itself. A dream. Nothing on trust.

Then I swivelled my own head a little. There was the world
caught as my glass had been caught, between held and not-
                                                         held:

the ash in my garden awake and bristled with spring,
its fistfuls of buds half-showing their soot-coloured wings;

new moss in the gutter; new haze of threadbare grass;
new crocus clumps plumping; new everything filled with the
                                                         grace

of life between nothing and something, filled with the sense
of learning again to belong, to be quickened by chance,

to be pitched once more through undoubtable air for the sake
of finding what next is in store, to fall, to see if I break.

Salt Water

The village of Orford, five miles south of Aldeburgh on the Suffolk coast, survived for centuries as a fishing port; now it is separated from the sea by the river Alde, and by a strip of land known as the Ness. The Ness is ten miles long, stretching from Slaughden to North Wear Point. It is overlooked by a twelfth-century castle, and is also known as the Spit and the Island.

During the First World War, the Armament Experiment Flight of the Central Flying School was stationed on the Ness, which became a site for parachute testing and, later, a firing and bombing range. In the late 1930s Orford Research Programme was founded, and the Ness became a Listening Post and a centre for experimental work on radar. It was later taken over by the Atomic Weapons Research Establishment, and laboratories were built in which the triggers for nuclear bombs were tested; these were closed down in 1971. The Ness was then cleared by the Explosive Ordnance Disposal Unit. It was sold to the National Trust in 1993.

In the reign of King Henry II, when the village still faced the sea, a local historian recorded the capture of the Orford Merman. This Merman was kept in the castle, where *whether he would or could not, he would not talk, although oft-times hung up by his feet and harshly tortured*. Eventually he was released into the harbour.

In the late eleven-fifties
when the river and the sea
were still in one another's arms
and lived in harmony

there came a summer day so hot
the sea seemed hardly wet,

[46]

and the fishermen remained at home
until the sun had set,

had set and rustled up a breeze
and high tide at the full,
so just like that their sails were out
beyond the harbour wall.

A mile offshore, before the shape
of home had slipped away,
they hushed, and cast their clever nets
like grain into the bay.

One hour passed. Another hour.
The house lights on the land
began to jitter and go out,
the darkness to expand,

and silence in a steady flood
rushed round them silkily,
and even filtered through their nets
to calm the rocking sea.

No iron-filing shoal of fish
criss-crossed the rock-strewn floor,
no oyster winked, no battling crab
stuck out an angry claw,

the clear-cut worlds which make the world
lost all their difference,
the sea was sky, deep down was high,
and nonsense seemed like sense.

Enough like sense, at least, to mean
that in the red-eyed dawn,
with courses set and sails poised
to catch the first wind home,

it seemed the sort of miracle
that no one thought was rare
for one of them to haul on board
his streaming net and there

to find a merman large as life —
a merman! — half death-pale,
half silver as a new-made coin
and fretted like chain-mail.

*

For a million years one life simply turns into the next —
the spider hangs between driftwood and sea holly,
the sparrow hawk balances exactly over a shrew,
the hare sits bolt upright and urgent, all ears:
there is no reason why any of this should change.

But a new thought arrives and the island is invaded —
a radio mast stands up and starts cleaning its whiskers,
a field of mirrors learns to see clear beyond the Alps,
a set of ordinary headphones discovers the gift of tongues:
there is no reason why any of this should change.

Work goes ahead smoothly but no one breathes a word —
a slim needle is sensibly embarrassed by the red,
a pressure gauge puffs out its cheeks but is always steady,

a bird-walk of mathematics knows just where it is going:
there is no reason why any of this should change.

*

Not rare? Not like a miracle?
No, not until he spoke,
when feebly as a rotten thread
the spell that held them broke

and every clear-cut bit of world
snapped back into its place:
the sea was sea, the sky was sky,
the merman's face his face,

which slid between its salty lips
an eel-dance of a tongue,
a tongue which could not fix or shape
the words it splashed among.

This made the fishermen afraid;
it told them they had caught
a devil deaf to every law
their own religion taught,

or else, perhaps, a different god
they could not understand
but had to honour and obey
when they returned to land.

*

To create an explosion is the point of all this,
an explosion neither too soon nor too late,

an explosion precisely where it needs to be,
over the head of an enemy.

Not yet.

Scientists arrive to test triggers for the explosion,
triggers which must boil like hell and also be frozen,
triggers which must shake themselves silly and still work,
still know how to create a vacuum.

Not yet.

Weird laboratories spring up for these triggers,
Chinese pagoda-roofs which will protect the triggers
and which in the case of an accident with the triggers
will collapse and bury everything.

Not yet.

But it turns out that the vacuum cannot wait to be born,
the vacuum feeds itself on the very idea of discovery,
the vacuum wants to swallow the whole village and show
the explosion might as well already be over.

Not yet.

*

They made their choice; they froze their hearts;
they bound the merman's wrists
and wound him tightly in their net
with clumsy turns and twists;

then swerved towards the shore again,
and just as sunlight came
above the crescent harbour wall
they brought their trophy home.

Wives and children crowded round,
mouths gaping with surprise,
and gaping back the merman cried
baleful, senseless cries,

cried tears as well as sighs and sobs,
cried gulps, cried gasps, cried blood,
cried out what sounded like his soul
but never cried a word.

This made the fishermen afraid
again, it made them guess
the merman might have come to them
to put them through a test

and they, by cruelly catching him,
marooning him in pain,
and putting him on show like this
had blundered into sin.

*

Then the triggers are ready, they neither boil
nor freeze, they spin at any speed you please,
and are carried off like gifts in velvet boxes.

Then the bomb disposal men pick to and fro
with their heads down, each one carefully alone
and quiet, like pioneers prospecting for gold.

Then the radio masts die, their keen whispers
and high songs go, their delicate necks bow,
and voices fill up the air without being heard,

Then the field of mirrors folds too, its flat glare
shatters and shuts up, cannot recall the highest Alp
or anything except types of cloud, come to that.

Then the waves work up a big rage against roof-tiles
and breeze blocks, against doors, ventilation shafts, clocks,
and moon-faced instrument panels no one needs any more.

Then the wind gets to work. It breaks into laboratories
and clapboard sheds, it rubs out everything everyone said,
clenching its fingers round door jambs and window frames.

Then the gulls come to visit, shuffling noisily
into any old scrap-metal mess, settling on this for a nest,
and pinning their bright eyes on bare sky overhead.

And in due season flocks of beautiful shy avocets –
they also come back, white wings scissored with black,
calling their wild call as though they felt human grief.

*

They wound a rope around his net
and dragged him through the square,
up the looming castle keep,
then down the castle stair

and down and down and down and down
through wet-root-smelling air

into a room more cave than room
and hung him there.

Not hung him up until he died,
but hung him by his tail,
his tail which shone like silver once
and crinkled like chain-mail,

then built a fire beneath his head
to see if he could learn
the language that he still refused,
plain words like *scare*, like *burn*,

and other words like *agony*,
like *hatred*, and like *death*,
though hour by hour not one of these
weighed down the merman's breath.

This made the fishermen afraid
once more; it made them see
that somehow they the torturers
had set their victim free.

*

The waves think their hardest task
is to work each stone into a perfect O;
the marram thinks all it must do
is hold tight and not trouble to grow.

There's no story, never a point of view,
there's nothing here that's trustworthy or true.

Each grain of salt thinks it is able to see
over the highest Alp with its pure white eye;
the sea holly thinks it alone
can support the whole weight of the sky.

There's no clue, never a word in your ear;
there's nothing here that's justified or clear.

Winter storms think they will bring
the worst news anyone can bear to be told;
the east wind thinks it can certainly blow
colder than the coldest possible cold.

There's no code, never an easy cure;
there's nothing here that's definite or sure.

*

They cut him down. They hauled him up
the whirlpool of the stair,
they dragged him past their wives and children
gawping in the square,

and silently, as though the words
they used to know before
were all dead now, they carried him
down to the shingle shore.

They slid him tail-first in the sea
and washed the bitter drops
of blood-crust from his finger ends
and salt-spit from his lips,

and all the while, still silently,
they watched the tide bring in
a brittle, dimpled, breaking flood
of silver through his skin,

then open up his glistening eyes
in which they saw their fear
rise up to greet them one last time
and fade, and disappear,

disappear while they stood back
like mourners round a grave,
and watched his life ebb out of theirs
wave by wave by wave.

PART TWO Sailing to Italy

*When John Keats first coughed blood, on 3 February 1820, he said
to his friend Charles Brown: 'I know the colour of that blood. It is
arterial blood. That drop of blood is my death warrant. I must die.'
Through the following spring, he was nursed at home in Hampstead
– and occasionally in London. His doctors bled him and put him on
a starvation diet; his condition deteriorated steadily. By the late
summer, it was decided that he should go to Rome, where the cli-
mate might do him some good.*

*He sailed for Naples from Tower Bridge on 17 September, taking
his friend the painter Joseph Severn as a companion. Their boat was
the* Maria Crowther, *a 127-ton, twin-masted, square-rigged brigan-
tine. It had six crew and two other passengers – a Mrs Pigeon and a
Miss Cotterell. Miss Cotterell was also consumptive, and joined
them at Gravesend on 18 September.*

By six in the evening, I've already packed. The children help me.
Bag for the ship, bag for ashore. 'Sea-bag, land-bag. Sea-bag,
land-bag.'

An April sunset – drizzling, and only three days to May Day.
Sparrows are fidgeting in the beech-tree below my bedroom
window. A thrush sings, its voice like loose change flung onto
the ground. Beyond it: traffic, a police siren, one boy shouting
and another calling back. I feel like a child myself; undefended.

First thing next morning – to St Katherine's Basin, by Tower
Bridge. The cab driver wants to know why.

'I'm sailing to Italy.'

'*Sailing* to Italy?'

I nod.

'Ever sailed before?'

'Only in the bath.'

I first see *Excelsior* from across the Basin – up to now, it's been photographs. Click: the slim black-painted hull. Click: the two paler masts. Now here they are in fact, but still implausible. Everything is so much smaller than I thought, so much more precarious and antiquated.

The moment I step on deck it's all right. Beautiful elaborate rigging – its names and functions unknown to me. The big brown sails all furled. Blue and red paint round the base of the tiller, on the capstan, on hinges. The ensign is tangled round a mast, and the deck worn pale with feet and sun and scrubbing brushes – the nail-heads and board-joints all plugged with pitch. I pace from end to end. Eighty feet. That's the same size as the *Maria Crowther* – though this is a fishing smack, not a brig.

I doodle round, meeting the crew. Stewart White, the skipper. A huge man, 50s, bald, with a fringe of thick grey hair. He was brought up in Sizewell on the Suffolk coast, where his father worked as a cowman on the cliffs overlooking the sea. Before the power station was built. 'We went there because my brother had asthma and our doctor told him to run wild and free.' He snaps his fingers. 'My brother was better in a year.'

Paul Collins, the mate: younger, moustache, ear-ring, tattoo of the ship on his right forearm.

Bill Ewan, bosun: red-bearded, pipe-smoking. A Scot – the only crew member who's not an East Anglian.

John Cooper, bosun's mate: a thick-set vole.

Clinton Hall, watchleader: smiling, weather-beaten, veiny face.

Claire Walker, second watchleader. Round glasses, soft

voice, smoking roll-ups. She seems unlike the others, more reserved.

Liz Blake, the cook: skirling laugh, florescent leggings. The others all wear jeans and brown smocks.

Paul takes me below to store my stuff. I have a forward cabin to myself – the top bunk full of life-belts, me below. There's a cupboard in one wall but it's packed with food. I can stand upright, and just turn round without touching the sides. My bunk is like a coffin – rough planks making the wall I'll sleep beside; the plywood base of the top bunk close to my face. I can stretch out straight, just.

Then Paul takes me through the rest of the ship. First the galley: a stove and sink in one corner, a central table with folding leaves, a row of paperbacks, six bunks let into two walls. There's also a clock and a barometer, and a copy of the Psalms and New Testament in a wooden mount inscribed 'Think on These Things'. Next, a heavy iron door to a corridor which leads past the skipper's cabin. The engine room and the chart room. I glimpse a radio, a telephone, dials, blank screens. After these, the crew's quarters in the horseshoe stern – dark dull wood, a small empty fireplace, six more bunks.

Climbing back on deck through the aft-hatch ('Mind your head') Paul tells me the ship was originally a trawler – built in Lowestoft in 1921, then re-built between 1985 and 1988. Once there were hundreds like her. Now she's the only one left. 'Back in the '80s there were dozens lost in a single night. There's a song about it. Stewart'll sing it to you.' He means the 1880s.

When I'm above ground again, the deck feels larger than at first – spacious, for all the coils of rope, the hatches and winches and rings, the main boom and the mizzen I have to keep ducking. Yet even here we are always in each other's way. The simplest movement is an elaborate exercise in courtesy and planning. 'No, after *you*.'

A foot-tall pink plastic duck is tied to a hatch in the centre of the deck. Claire tells me it's called Sophy – fished out of the sea years ago because it reminded Stewart of a blonde he once knew. Apparently *Excelsior* sails best when Sophy is facing into the wind.

There's a slow fidgety potter and the dock-bridges lift in the sunlight – one brown, one red, one white. We tie up and wait for the last to open. The ship feels like a race-horse waiting for the start. Shining harness and strength held back.

Then the white bridge lifts and out we slide – into the Thames. Tower Bridge to my right is so suddenly and starkly itself, it might be the lid of a giant biscuit tin.

With the engine pushing us downstream, and the current pressing us inland, we hover in the broad middle of the river. Sunlight and cold wind. Dazzle. My chest tightens as the crew begin hoisting the sails, releasing a slick of rain water at the final stretch. The tackle leaves snaky wet-prints on the deck.

I sit in the stern. Stewart takes a hefty rope and ties the brass throat of the tiller first from one side, then the other, keeping us steady. A man waving on the dockside by the Basin entrance is immediately tiny. The second time I look back, I can't be sure whether he is still there or not. Yet it is I who feel invisible.

The tide turns and we pick up speed. St Paul's winks at me through the centre of Tower Bridge. To left and right are more-or-less familiar things. Butler's Wharf; the churches and restaurants I know; the embankment walks and restored streets; the modern dockland. There's a sense of holiday, of larking about. I am seeing old things from a new angle, but it won't last long. Soon I will return to my familiar life.

It does last. Within a few moments I'm disorientated, the wind blowing in my face. My eyes water, blurring the derelict docks turned into marinas. The puzzling geometries of cement. Occasionally a small hovercraft hums past; sometimes three or four barges tied together, full of rubbish. Around and between all these things, the river is completely empty. Its slow sprawl seawards from Tower Bridge is a story of things thinning and decaying. It is the life running out of the country.

I go below to collect lunch, then angle it back on deck. We're passing Greenwich – I recognise this! There's the Trafalgar pub and the *Cutty Sark*. I've visited here, walking and looking. I've even walked *under* here, through Greenwich Tunnel. I want us to stop, so I can fit everything into my mind carefully and remember it later, but the current is fast now, and whisks me away before I finish looking.

It's 4.30 when we pass the first open field. We left at 2.30. Then another two hours and we reach Gravesend, where the *Maria Crowther* stopped, Severn bought Keats some laudanum, and the Captain got off to try and find a goat for their voyage. Behind the low frontage, the slipway and the supermarket, the dark-red brick church tower appears – the church they would have seen. I wait for its clock to chime seven, but nothing happens.

On deck again after supper, what's left of the day yawning emptily. The river isn't like a river at all now. On one side, a shoreline of stubby refinery drums; on the other, a long concrete wall with a beard of black weed. The wind has steadied. Again and again, cold rose light flashes across the water, then bounces back to the sky. I feel spellbound. At last it has started.

18–19 September. Keats leaves Gravesend and sails into the Thames estuary. Heavy winds drive the Maria Crowther *past Margate and Dover. After breakfast on the 19th, all the passengers are ill and take to their bunks for the day.*

The water makes two noises against the planks of my cabin wall. One a long hissing plunge as the prow rises and falls through the waves, the other a cosy gurgle – an intimate sound, pressing inside my ear. When I turned in yesterday, we were still at the mouth of the Thames. I lay awake until 2, hearing the weather worsen. Every noise seemed magnified. Weird snaffling heaves. Brutal flappings and scrapings. Was something wrong? Surely someone would tell me.

I dreamed I was on a bare-topped barge – a huge old metal hulk – stuck tight in a frozen river. My children were playing on the ice, which I saw was suddenly breaking up, so they scrambled back on board. The entire river-way immediately melted and we set off terrifyingly fast, hurtling towards a brilliant light. I thought we'd never slow down. Then the river took an impossible swerve uphill – a slow winding hill – and by the time we reached the summit we were at a dead stop. We climbed down and found a warreny village of dark-gold stone. It looked expensive and comfortable but we were not welcome. Doors closed in our faces. Windows were locked against us. I felt resentful but at the same time liberated. We walked close together, leaving the village for open country.

Dawn at 5. Margate. Keats stayed here a couple of times, lying on the cliff top ('clift top') and writing. From this distance all I can see is a mishmash of Georgian façades, amusement halls, shut fish-and-chip shops. In the silent fairground behind the front, wet cars shine on the Ferris wheel.

We're two hours behind schedule – it's blowing too hard. I put myself in the stern, and watch the waves build and collapse into oily hollows. Every few minutes one crashes over the side, streams across deck, and shudders away through the bilges.

At Ramsgate they take in the sails. A big fist of wind punches the mainsail as it's lowered, dragging it through its restraining rope so it smashes violently to and fro, raking across the deck. I'm already so used to strangeness, it takes a moment to realise something has gone wrong. Then Paul is shouting 'Fuck! Mind your heads! Fuck! Fuck!' and clawing his way up the rigging, apparently treading on air. I can't see how, but he makes things safe, shouting orders to the rest of the crew. Then he jumps down on deck again, grim-faced, running both hands over his hair.

Stewart turns to me: 'Well, that's this morning's excitement over.'

'Cup of tea, I think,' says Paul.

We blunder on towards Brighton.

*

Two things are happening at once, one telling me I am where I am, the other cutting me loose.

The wind chafes and frets, puddling rain off my oilskins, gluing me onto the ship and demanding I understand what all this equipment means and does. The detail is bewildering: the two masts with their ropes branching like a half-open, wind-stripped umbrella. The tackle worn smooth and gleaming. The sails with their machine-gun holes for reefing and binding. It is a complete world, packed and self-sufficient.

But all afternoon, as the weather lifts and Brighton fades behind us, I look more and more towards the open sea. There are no details out there – none that I can recognise yet, anyway. Just pure openness. A bright nothing I can't enter. It is the opposite of a world, everything the ship has to compete with and overcome.

Imagine everything you know
stops dead. Imagine winds don't blow.
Imagine waves like oily skin
and clouds not moving, tissue-thin.
Imagine heat trapped in the sun.
Imagine blood which cannot run.

[65]

Imagine heartbeats marking time
in time, no longer part of time.
Imagine everything you see
beginning its beginning endlessly.

After supper the wind dies altogether. A beautiful, calm, back-lit evening, with silver mist coming on. I unwind my fishing lines from the stern and let myself drift away. No one can reach me now; I can reach no one.

Later still, on deck watching the stars: the whole uninterrupted sky in a single glance, immaculate and magnified. Even so, I can't work out the constellations. They must have been desperate in those days, to see this was a belt and that a bear.

20 September. The Maria Crowther *is off Brighton. A calm sea, but wind from the south-west indicates a storm approaching. It reaches them in mid-afternoon, blowing full in their faces. The ship begins to leak, Keats's cabin is flooded, and the Captain veers round and runs twenty miles back the way they have come, to Dungeness.*

May day. When I come on deck, Stewart says we're in Haslar, round the harbour from Portsmouth. I've never heard of Haslar. It's a marina – a jigsaw of different whitenesses. White veil of cloud overhead, very high and thin. White light on the water. White gin-palaces tethered in line beside us, all deserted, none moving in the early heat. They might be bundles of money.

I want strangeness – not this dead calm and prosperity.

Stewart is re-tying the ribbon which holds Sophy to the hatch-lid, as if he were thinking the same thing. Open sea. 'You'll be safe here', he says, meaning on the ship, not in the harbour. 'There's no storm that can sink her. Rocks, that's another thing. But not weather'.

Has he ever been in danger?

'I fell overboard a couple of times. Both times I was fishing. It was off Lowestoft. I just went to pull in my nets, slipped, and over I went. You wouldn't believe how fast boats go, even when they're not moving'. He rubs his face. 'I'm strong enough, but that boat . . . I kicked my boots off, I can tell you, but when I caught up, all I could do was cling on. Just hang there. I knew I only had one chance to get back on board, you see. But I did it. Here I am.'

And the other time?

'The other time I got caught in the nets, that's what saved me.' He rubs his face again. 'I hate the taste of salt water.'

By mid-morning, no cloud and the sun beating down. Mediterranean heat. We're waiting for provisions but they won't come, and don't come till afternoon. In ordinary life, so much empty time would seem enormous. Here it doesn't matter. The things which seem like events – making coffee, eating lunch – are all over in a moment. But the things which seem like nothing take hours, and fill up the day. Watching the shore complicate as the heat builds (there's a submarine dangling in mid-air outside the museum in the harbour). Trying to work out which rope, tied to which block, works which sail.

I drifted out yesterday. Now I am further off still. Gentle rocking. The rigging creaking whenever the wake of a passing boat shifts us. It's the sound of something gradually tightening round my head, intense but painless, putting me to sleep.

Not the thrush at evening
tip-top the holly bush,
showering the ground
with its loose-change song,

no, but the herring gull
with its wing-sails full,
catching a free ride
on the air's blue high tide.

21 September. Keats is off Dungeness, becalmed. He goes ashore, walking on the shingle beach, then returns to the Maria Crowther *in the evening. He is weak and irritable, resenting the ailing Miss Cotterell.*

There's a smell of mice in my cabin. Not mice. Me.

We sail from Haslar at 10 – the gin palaces squeaking as we disturb them – and pass HMS *Warrior* on the opposite shore, its huge masts rigged like pylons.

It's another baking day, we're all in T-shirts and barefoot, and the crew seem tetchy. They want real weather and something to do. 'This is just yachting,' one of them says.

Even so, the ship still feels higgledy-piggledy – everyone in everyone's way. Walking to the bow means first seeing who wants to come aft, then making accelerated dashes from tiller to hatch-top to capstan, remembering not to trip over that rope, this hook, that iron bar screwed to the deck ('It's not an *iron bar* – it's a horse,' says Stewart, 'A *horse*.')

And going below decks is the same. It means planning, calling, checking, calling again. I am a child, finding easy things difficult, learning what is ordinary.

Except that nothing stays ordinary. Within half an hour the land behind us is drowned in a milky mist – the pretty cupola of Portsmouth Cathedral is the last thing to disappear. Then the Isle of Wight begins to emerge ahead: caravans outside Cowes; what looks like a fortified hotel at Yarmouth; scruffy woods coming down to the shore where a woman is walking her dog.

We have to dock at Yarmouth tonight – I want to spend tomorrow on the island – but the afternoon is ours for what we want.

So along the coast we go, tacking in a dozy zigzag, as close as we dare to Hurst Castle in mid-channel. There's a skyline of crumbling yellow stone, and the gun emplacements, built by some long-ago Henry – I can't remember – look as functional as garage doors. Sea gulls float in and out of their darkness. A cormorant stands bolt upright on the rocks below: an exclamation mark.

There's no wind but the tide takes us, and as we pass the castle it floats off like a transfer in its watery sky-bowl. I think: that's it for today, we'll turn back in a moment, but the Needles appear – I'd forgotten about them. The smooth green ramp of the island raises its launching pad, bristling and climbing and keeping going – and then . . . Then nothing. No, not quite nothing. Three more stuttering chalk footprints. And then nothing – this time spreading all the way to the horizon.

The lighthouse isn't working yet, it just stands there looking banal and clumsy in the late evening light. All the same, we use it as a marker and start back to Yarmouth. While we do this, as though someone has thrown a switch, the tide turns and a wonderful wide O of water appears beside us, ringed by turbulent waves as the currents clash and resolve.

When we pass Hurst Castle again this circle is still visible, and I catch myself imagining the head of a sea monster might erupt from its centre and snarl at us. Even after so few days, even so close to land, it's easy to imagine history including mysteries, and mysteries breeding myths.

22–27 September. The Maria Crowther *flounders slowly along the south coast, passing Brighton for the second time.*

Keats came to the Isle of Wight twice: I want to see his places. But leaving *Excelsior* where we anchored last night, and driving from Yarmouth to Shanklin Chine in the south-east, I feel him slipping away – the solid ground swaying as if I were still at sea, the whole island barred and bolted against me. Tightly bound parcels of grazing. Villages hunched over themselves. Kitschy gift-shops selling little framed postcard-poems: 'To a Grandmother'; 'To a Pussy' (rhymes with 'fussy'). When I am on the ship, nowhere, I am close to him without thinking about him. Here he can't keep his place.

Not even in the Chine. 'The wondrous Chine', he called it – 'a very great Lion' – but even in his day it had been stared into stiffness. 'I wish I had as many guineas as there have been spy glasses in it', he said. There is the same long-falling but thin waterfall that he would have seen, the same over-arching trees, the same drowsy pigeon notes. Did their ancestors watch him here, making the steep climb? It's beautiful, but nothing gives him away.

And again at Carisbrooke, where an ant-army of schoolchildren are on a school trip. I stroll along the castle wall above the village where he stayed. A man in shorts is nailing up bunting outside a pub to celebrate VE Day. A shop window is a kaleidoscope of Union Jacks.

By 6 I'm back at the harbour. The day feels a failure – except that as soon as I step on board I find him waiting for me. More than that. I am at home here. I am beginning to know what things mean.

As we sail past Hurst Castle and the Needles again (they look clumpier now, and Liz thinks it would be better to call them the Molars) the sun sets in a brilliant orange sludge and the moon zings up immediately. It's only a slim crescent, but makes a wide stripe on the water.

Bournemouth slides away, a cheerful Lucozade colour.

Then supper, and Paul tells me about a storm he once sailed through off Denmark. Coming on deck he saw a vast wave behind them – overwhelmingly high – but it squeezed underneath and *Excelsior* surfed down its face like a dolphin. He makes a wobbling gesture with one hand, going 'Whoosh, whoosh, whoosh. Three-hundred-ton wave. If that lot had landed on us we'd have gone down.'

I fall asleep thinking of Keats missing his family – not just Fanny Brawne. His brother George who married and went to America. His sister – also called Fanny – incarcerated with a guardian. Their dead brother Tom. There's a story of Keats playing cricket once and getting a black eye; perhaps the children sometimes played cricket together in the early days? All the boys, anyway.

It's 1812, and their parents are both dead.
The Keats brothers are playing cricket: George bowling,
John at the crease, Tom (who will be the first to die)
at mid-off with the sun in his eyes, seeing stars.

George runs in, it's short, John takes a heave,
and as luck would have it connects very sweetly,
so the ball (which for some reason is white)
travels in a steadily rising line and straight

through Tom's outstretched fingers, leaving a faint
sensation of burning, gathering speed as it goes,
lifting clear over a line of skinny poplars
which have their hair on end and mark the boundary

not just of the pitch but of the countryside itself,
dividing it from London, where the boys once lived,

and over which now the cricket ball is still
carrying and brightly visible – a pure white dot

glowing and dropping a few flakes of fire
onto the roofs, graveyards and gardens below,
which means anyone there who might suddenly glance up
would surely say *God! A new star! Or maybe a planet?*

Up at dawn the next morning to see Lulworth Cove. I've often
visited here, but today I don't know where I am. It's lunar grey in
the early mist. On one bulbous hill, caravans flash their chain-
mail. In the cove itself a black fuzz of trees and a fishing boat
riding at anchor. I think of what I know: of Hardy, of the tour-
ists, of the army here (our chart warns us they sometimes fire out
to sea). But none of these things, none of these people connect
with it now. It is only itself – the slowly darkening green plates
slipping into and over each other; the deserted shore turning
over its stones; the sea slithering through cold holes in the chalk.

'Seen enough?' says Stewart, flapping his arms to keep warm.
'All right, then.'

The crew re-set the sails and as we slide west towards
Weymouth the mist burns away. All along the coast, sea-shapes
repeat in the wave-patterns of the cliffs.

Last night, at supper in the galley, we heard Stewart on deck
playing his squeeze-box and singing. When I ask him about it
now he gives an embarrassed laugh. 'Well, I sing in the pubs
round Suffolk, you know,' he says, 'when I'm not doing this'. He
pats the tiller. 'I've got hundreds of songs – folk songs, that is.
They don't mean so much until you've been to sea. I mean –
they're all true. You can learn things from them. I don't read
poetry but I reckon they're poetry.' He opens and shuts his
hands as if he's playing. Enormous splayed hands. His big head
with its monkish fringe of hair.

It's hotter than ever today – freakishly hot. In the afternoon I lie on deck and topple into and out of sleep: the ship rocking forward, wind running down the sails in useless ripples, the engine puttering. Everything we pass on shore, the villages on tiptoe at the cliff edge, the smooth fields where cattle keep their heads down – all these things begin and end in the same instant. I can't get a purchase on them.

With Stewart again. 'And I'll tell you another thing. See this?' This means the radar, which lives in the hatch in front of the tiller. Liquid crystals flicker at the foot of the screen, telling us the depth of the water we're sailing through, and bands of blue, red and yellow confirm it, and show whether the sea-bed is soft or rocky. 'I can tune it to find fish,' Stewart says. 'See?' Immediately, a rag of red flaps into the blue. Mackerel – bunching together, then away in a fraying comet's tail. 'What do you think? Better put out your lines. You never know.'

After supper I catch eight in one haul and the crew are surprisingly excited. For me, perhaps.

Another furious, squashy sunset – melting orange and purple scarves – then darkness at one bound.

*

By morning we're off Teignmouth and have to stoodge around waiting for high water so we can enter the harbour. Russet cliffs tumbling into choppy water. The town is another model village from this distance: Lego houses, a church, the Ness curling round to shelter the docks. I catch more mackerel and we have them for breakfast, rolled in oats.

When Keats nursed his brother Tom here in 1818 it rained almost continuously. He called it 'a splashy, rainy, misty, snowy, foggy, haily, floody, muddy, slipshod country'. Today it's cloudless, and when I go ashore to visit the place he stayed, everyone's in shirt-sleeves and dark glasses.

There's no trace of him in his house: new windows, the façade re-covered, his room a plain cube filled with the present owner's Indian rugs and statues.

I drive to a heath overlooking the harbour. Is he here instead? I stare and stare. The details change so much more quickly than at sea. Last year's bracken burnt-out and flaking. New bracken uncurling its baby squid-arms. A clump of intense violets. All this feels too familiar to release him from his life into mine.

When I get back to the ship I'm ready to leave at once, but we can't. High tide is at 10 tomorrow – we'll have to wait.

I lie in my cabin, trying to think what it will mean to lose sight of land. Today in Teignmouth, the other day on the Isle of Wight, I have been in touch with more-or-less usual things. With schedules and deadlines. With the idea of home. At the same time I've been losing them. The photograph of a cruise ship comes into my head, and streamers flung down by the departing passengers to people waving them off on the quay. When the streamers break, the journey begins. It's like that. All week the coastline has been like a long ribbon held in my hand – a ribbon tied at its far, invisible end to London and everyday things, but all the time tightening and wearing out, humming with tension.

Tomorrow I shall simply let go.

*

What is the date today? I want to know. 6 May says Stewart, counting on his thick fingers. It doesn't seem to mean anything but I repeat it. 6 May. The day I leave England.

I've taken my place in the stern by 9.30, watching the crew set to work. Hauling ropes. Unfurling sails. People are calling out to us from the harbour wall – people I don't know. As we leave the entrance to the harbour, a family clambers into a blow-up dinghy and race out to circle us, red-faced and laughing. We wave down to them solemnly.

Solemnly. The mood is already different, even though we're still close to the shore. More serious. A suppressed excitement and anxiety.

The harbour master at Teignmouth has given Stewart two brill which he fillets on a hatch-lid, then sluices with sea water he pulls up in a metal bucket. He talks about the local council elections last Thursday. 'I don't care what colour people vote – red, blue, yellow. I just want people to speak their minds.'

A huge murky jellyfish slides past – the phallic dome and unfinished-looking rest of it. And another cormorant – the sunlight so bright on its beak, it looks as though it's carrying a fish.

Then I start fishing. Twenty-four mackerel in an hour. Moon-coloured bellies, black heads, the iridescent green-blue-black on the top of the body. The efficiency of their design!

In the early evening, at Start Point, we begin to leave the land behind. A mist wraps it first, cloaking a school of small sailing boats. Then a lighthouse starts – the juddering flash seeming to throw the whole head of land out to sea. One moment when I look back, the hills are still there, half-lit. When I look again, only a second later, they've gone.

Now the entire world is the boat – nothing else – creaking forward so slowly we might actually be standing still.

Three gulls have found a shoal of fish and are battering the surface, plunging and popping up gobbling. Liz the cook throws out some peelings and more gulls arrive, circling the rubbish, swooping to collect a piece, climbing, and dropping it when they discover it's inedible.

A big shining log drifts past with another seagull perched on top as though it's standing to attention. Stupid bird.

Just as the light is fading we pass two more cormorants, sitting side by side in the middle of nowhere, going nowhere. My heart swells and slows down. The cormorants pay no attention to us and have soon disappeared.

Supper and in my cabin by 9.30. I spin my radio dial just to hear what there is to hear, and all the voices that reach me sound frantic, urban, unbearable. Then I lie in the dark, asking myself unnecessary questions to make myself fall asleep. For instance: exactly what colour are the sails on this ship? Red? Brown? Blood? Liver? Tan? Tan. But something to do with fire as well – like the line of fire at the edge of a piece of burning paper. I roll this round my mind and it takes me back to my last birthday, then forward to now again. The sense of being neither here nor there.

The air on my birthday weighed much more,
even bringing me down to my knees once,
so the blank sheet I should have been writing on
flipped out of my hand into the fire and caught.

I felt my ghost beginning to take shape inside me –
a shrug through my whole body, a mirror-flash –
and its spongy eyes swivelling round to discover
the low-ceilinged room where it will one day live.

The flames curled through the white in a steady line,
driving before them a narrow brown band
which was no longer paper and not yet fire
but the in-between where things give up or start.

*

My first morning with no sight of land.

A pigeon has joined us – a battered-looking lost thing – a racer with one pale green ring and one turquoise. Clinton gives it some water and bread, but the others surround it and say they're going to eat it. The pigeon puffs out its breast feathers, cocks its head, and inspects them with a glittering brown eye.

Maybe it only speaks French, someone says. The pigeon stamps in its water bowl, then strolls around the deck shitting.

When will we reach the Bay of Biscay? Never at this slow rate. I have a sense of Biscay as a place, but wouldn't know I was there unless someone told me. It's a place which is not a place. I feel like a fly walking down a window-pane.

9.30. Wind building slowly. The catspaws filling in, so now the whole surface of the sea is ruffled. Bill is sand-papering the white deck-rail, which he's about to paint. I've gutted and filleted the mackerel for lunch.

Somebody says: the wonderful thing about sailing is you never know what's going to happen next. For most of today, nothing happens next. The pigeon attempts a few departures, circles the ship, and returns. The conversations on deck also circle and return. At 10.30 there's an astonishing CRACK out of the blue. Concorde breaking the sound barrier – we see its vapour trail curving away west.

We have planned to make 100 miles a day, and when I ask Stewart how we're doing, he tells me the engine broke last night. He seems puzzled but not worried by this. 'Never mind. We'll fix it.' Should *I* be worried? Various members of the crew disappear at intervals into the engine room; there's the sound of tinkering; then they emerge again, shrugging. Paul holds a bit of the engine and rubs it with a towel. 'We've got a week,' Stewart says. 'Time to build a new engine if need be.' With what, I wonder.

Standing in the bow, I watch a rib of dark something slipping towards us. Weed? Debris? It's a stick, shaped like a longbow, turning gently over and over in the swell so it's not like a stick any more, but a bobbin. A bobbin bob-bob-bobbin' along. And occasionally small cuttlefish slither past – miniature deserted surf-boards.

The line of the horizon hardens, and people say this means

lower air pressure, and rain. There's no sign of it. After lunch I fall asleep, and wake to find one mackerel has attached itself to my line. I fish in earnest for a while, but there's nothing doing.

Still drowsy by evening, when I realise I've got a sore throat. Mysteriously, it goes after a couple of hours, and I talk to Liz on deck, watching a fog creep up behind us. One minute there's sun and warmth, the next wetness, semi-darkness, the sea gun-metal with no depth. Stewart appears with a fog-horn – a big brown box like an old-fashioned projector. When he winds the handle it gives an alarmed moaning. I think of the bottle-top lowings I heard off the Isle of Wight – and beyond them of lying in bed in Hull nearly twenty years ago, hearing the buoys on the river Humber.

I roll into bed full of the sadness of that time, and try to banish it by listening to the radio again. Chirac is the new President of France. The Queen has opened the VE Day celebrations. These pieces of news reach me like reports from Mars.

God above, the sadness of the noises
reaching from the darkened middle distance!

Take just now the slapping of that sail
as wind falls wearily against its slope;

or take the dwindling din a tin bowl makes
as someone knocks it out with steady taps;

or take the flap-crash of a fish that shows
in fading circles where it lunged and rose.

All definite, all part of history,
and none of them the least to do with me!

Sea much rougher tonight. My sleeping-bag is made of some slippy stuff which makes me slither around with every roll and dip. It's easiest to lie on my back, but when I've done this for an hour, and still no sleep, I turn onto my right and wedge against the side-board of my bunk. My head still rocks, though – as if it is separate from the rest of me. Over onto my back again.

Suddenly there's a clinking and mad whipping sound overhead, which gives me a spurt of panic. Then quiet again: the sense of rushing forward, of plunging speed, but I know it's not fast really. I try not to think about how much black water there is beneath me, how far we are from land, but Ruth comes into my mind, and my grandmother, both drowned. Falling asleep, I suppose I wouldn't make any effort to escape, if water burst down the hatches.

28 September. Still no favourable wind. The Maria Crowther *puts in at Portsmouth for 24 hours. Keats goes ashore and visits his friends John and Laetitia Snook, at Bedhampton, near Chichester. He hears that Charles Brown is visiting nearby, but doesn't have time to meet him and returns to the* Maria Crowther *the following day.*

'Well, you're in it now,' says Stewart when I come on deck. He means the Bay of Biscay – and it's only two days since we left Devon. I look around, as if I expected to see a sign. The sky has lifted, but not much, the sea is the same as yesterday, only more developed. The slow swell is now a large sullen shrug, each wave carrying us several feet forward even though the following wave tries to suck us back. And the deck lies at a steep angle, with sudden twisting lurches. Now and then, without warning, breakers crash over the sides and wither away through the bilges.

John comes to talk. He tells me he's 59, and this is his last deep-sea voyage. He has a wife and two children near Norwich, in a house he bought twenty-odd years ago with money earned in Australia. He says he likes books about hoboes, especially W. H. Davies. His wide, impatient face. 'Are you enjoying it? It's no good thinking of home – there's nothing you can do about it, or it about you. You just have to sit here and watch it all slip past.'

The foghorn has disappeared from deck – and the pigeon. I wonder who killed it.

At breakfast, Paul starts talking about Bosnia. 'If there is a God, I think he's Jehovah, making us suffer unto the sixth and seventh generation.' He has a way of looking down and away when he's saying something important, stroking the inside of his left arm with his right hand. 'Sometimes I don't think we deserve to survive, we species known as Man.' His hair flops round his face and he lunges forward to fork down bacon and slippery fried egg.

A tanker inches across the horizon, heading back to England. Our wake, which yesterday looked like the track of a steam iron through clothes, is now a quick turbulent trace stippled with foam.

Where is Keats in all this? Our lives are so far apart. I can't go back home and find him, full of news. But I can look at the sea and imagine what it made him feel. Emptiness. The wide wilderness of water. Monotony of the waves. These are all things which stop time, and turn each different moment into the same moment, each hour into one that could equally well be the hour before or the hour after, it doesn't matter. And simultaneously: the knowledge of moving forward. The flotsam drifting past. The knots of weed. A plank from a broken crate. All these say: the future is waiting, landfall is waiting, death is waiting.

Noon. We've made 86 miles in the last 24 hours, but the wind is building now, and colder, which means we may make up some time. All the same, it's fickle and fluky: the ship judders, sprinting for a moment then stalled, the sails whipped full then hanging slack again. It's queasy-making; stupefying. Nobody comes on deck except the watch, who take it in half-hour turns to work the tiller. They check the compass, housed in the hatch in front of them at knee height, every few minutes – then adjust the tiller and sit down on the rope which holds it, keeping the course steady.

By mid-afternoon we've reached the continental shelf, where the sea bed dives from 80-odd metres down to four miles. If it were earlier in the year we'd see whales here, feeding on the plankton which teem upwards as the cold deep meets the warmer current. I hang over the black water – darkness packed solid beneath me. Nothingness. Then I look up. White horses shamble past aimlessly. A red-and-black tanker, going three times our speed. A gannet cresting the swell, then flipping airborne, inspecting us, before it planes away into the distance. It is an event for us; we are nothing to it.

Do the crew love being at sea so much because their lives on land are disappointing? They never talk about home, or, if they do, speak stiltedly. Stewart says, 'Oh well; I live in Lowestoft. I just don't . . . I can't see the sea from my house'.

I stand with my back to the main mast, looking straight ahead, and find myself thinking of Soho. Now is about the time I might be going out to supper. Bustle and bright windows. Stepping off the pavement into the street because there are so many people. Blares of music. Dog shit. Glossy heaps of bin-bags. In Keats's day there were still open fields and huntsmen coursing hares. I don't want to be there – I want to be here. But I miss it.

In a level meadow
skirting the city

the huntsman hollas
So-ho! So-ho!

Streets step forward
to stamp out the grazing,

clouds sink down
weeping brick dust and slate,

and a madcap hare
bolts from the blue

to end his days
in a print under tissue,

a zigzag of milk
dribbled in coffee,

the terrified eye
of a dragon from China,

the brindled bush
some prick works through

with his mouth half asleep
and the girl's too:

Sooo-hooo! Sooo-hooo!

In my bunk by 9. Still vaguely light, but no more point in the day. Last night as soon as darkness fell there were streaks of phosphorescence in the water, and spangling stars on deck – the plankton fretted into brilliant life. Tonight we're too far from land, and there's none.

I turn the dial on my radio once again, running through all the stations, trying all the frequencies. I get a snatch of French, of Spanish, a buzzy riff of rock-and-roll. Otherwise just the rush of empty space, and the slap-dribble-slap of waves against my cabin wall.

29 September. The Maria Crowther *sails from Portsmouth, past Yarmouth on the Isle of Wight, past the Needles, and along the Dorset coast towards Lulworth.*

I forgot to say: last night I helped set a different (larger) jib. Taking down the old one was like felling a tree: a soft rattling crash and the sky suddenly empty. The new sail seemed comforting as soon as we had it up – shelter as well as energy.

This morning the wind has worked round to the east and we've changed tack. Still cold, still grey without rain, the ship sailing a little more evenly. All the same, it could be yesterday. Or the day before.

Paul hung a bucket over the side to sluice down the deck, and brought up a crab, pale green, which lay on its back wriggling, then got booted over the side. What did it think had happened to it, snatched from its mid-Biscay existence for a moment? A glimpse of the afterlife.

Long, blank morning, which suddenly comes alive round mid-day. The wind drops, the sun bursts out, and we hit a big shoal of mackerel. Twenty in half an hour, some around 2 lbs. I stop when there's enough for supper, and as I'm cleaning them over the side a French turbo-prop, checking on fishing boats, drones very low over us from the west. We can see the pilot in his cockpit – bareheaded, moustached, and grinning. Everyone waves and bellows about fishing quotas as it drenches us with its racket. When it has disappeared into the pale south, there's an awkward silence – as though we're embarrassed to have shown ourselves pleased to see a new face.

Afternoon. Start reading *Don Juan*. Keats read Books 1 and 2 on his voyage, protesting that Byron made gay things solemn and solemn things gay. The poem is exactly fitted to annoy him. Its mockery of hoping that posterity will bring what life denies. Its laughter at lovesick youths who fill landscapes with gods and goddesses.

I carry on reading for hours, sitting on the lifeboat-case astern, my feet on the tiller-shaft where it sinks through a hole into the sea. The water here is brilliantly clear, catching the light off the keel, which is ochre.

Occasional conversations. With Bill, who worked on an oil rig off the Faroes for a while, made enough money to buy a six-bedroom house, then gave up. 'There were 90–odd people on that rig and only two I'd want to have a drink with ashore. You might think I'm a bit rough, but you should see them.' He lights his pipe with the blowtorch he's using to melt pitch. Bits of his beard catch fire and he pats himself out.

At some stage it occurs to me that I've never been so bored in my life. But I don't want to be anywhere else, doing anything else. My boredom isn't painful – it's like a trance, a rapture. Sometimes I feel as though I've been taken out of myself and am floating round the ship like Ariel. At others, as though my brain were lying on a wooden slab and shallow water sloshing over it, wearing me down to a sliver. My fishing line droops off the stern, and when I tweak and release it I think I'm fishing for minutes. I never catch one. The indifferent sun is glued to its place in the sky. My wristwatch has fallen asleep.

'Bloody Odin has let us down,' says Stewart, heaving into his orange jacket – 'Port of Felixtowe' fading across the back, kapok leaking from one elbow.

Supper at 6.30 – a relief to have something to do, but it passes in near silence and by 7 it's over. Stewart produces his squeeze-box and sings 'Fiddler's Green'. The squeeze-box has silver filigree work at either end, and tiny keys – it's almost impossible for his big fingers to hit only one note at a time. His voice is slightly nasal and heavily Suffolk-accented. Even the jolly songs sound melancholy, fading into vacancy.

To bed but no sleep. The near-calm means the mainsail makes a new whining creak, very loud. Around it are other, smaller noises – one a little escalating moan like someone fucking. It reminds me of a time towards the end of last year, when I suddenly heard my neighbour through the wall at home, shouting at his child. I'd turned on the radio, and was waiting for the news; the ceasefire in Northern Ireland had just been announced.

Adrift at home at six o'clock
I heard my neighbour through the wall

– *So eat, so eat your fucking meal!* –
and thought that if he'd just shut up

he'd catch the beeps before the news
and then the sound of news itself

from my side, drifting through to him
and due to start, and due to start . . .

He did shut up. I sat dead still.
The early dark drew in a breath

and held it. Silence fell. Or would
have done except that in the wall

a something could not help itself
and slipped: an idle plaster-crumb;

an avalanche; the silver whoosh
of wings above my head, then gone.

*30 September. Still calm. Keats goes ashore at intervals: Studland,
Holworth, Lulworth. He writes to Charles Brown about Fanny
Brawne, the woman he loves and has left behind in Hampstead.
'The thought of leaving Miss Brawne is beyond everything horrible –
the sense of darkness coming over me – I eternally see her figure
eternally vanishing. Some of the phrases she was in the habit of
using during my nursing at Wentworth Place ring in my ears – Is
there another life? Shall I awake and find all this a dream? There
must be – we cannot be created for this sort of suffering.'*

Eventually, in the early morning, I fall asleep for a few hours,
then wake up bleary and irritable. My shoulder aches; my hair
is filthy and itchy. We've spent part of the night going
backwards, and even though there's some wind now, it's only
inching us forward. The crew seem adamant the engine can't be
mended, though won't go into details about what's wrong with
it. 'You'll just have to chew fat.' 'You must have contingency
plans.' There's no point getting angry about this; there's
nothing anyone can do.

A gannet drifts past, then climbs and dives. It looks almost as
big as yesterday's aeroplane!

The crew show a kind of resigned facetiousness about our
delay. Paul throws some money into the waves. 'That's for
Neptune. I reckon there must be a fortune down there.' All that
happens is two more tankers appear. Behind them, bulbous rain
clouds drag along the horizon, keeping pace with us. The
treacly swell. A rag of lavatory paper, tied to the rigging to
show the direction of the wind, flutters its white flag. Jesus God,
it's still only 10.30.

Just before lunch Paul notices one of the fishing lines is heavy in the water and starts hauling it in. It's a shark – a young one – silvery on top like a jet fighter as it lashes towards us through the water, meek white underneath when it rolls over. We winch it on board, still writhing and toiling, giving off a faint smell of ammonia.

There's great jostling and jockeying as everyone crowds round, tries not to get flailed, snaps off photographs. The wide mirthless mouth, dragged open by the hook, looks senile. Liz sticks her head out of the fore-hatch and says she won't cook it. Paul puts on a pair of thick gloves and seizes it by the tail; the hook falls out of its mouth. 'It's a thresher,' says Stewart, pointing to the long tail fin.

As Paul lowers it back overboard, I glance beyond him into the flat sea – and a whale appears, a 100 yards or so from the stern. The immense oily back, the spout exploding upwards from the blowhole with a world-weary moan. When it subsides, it leaves a circle of dead calm. Somebody shouts 'There she blows!' – the phrase children used as a joke and now is nothing but the truth. Paul drops the shark back into the water where it lies still and stunned for a second, then whiplashes its whole body and melts into the blue.

The rest of the afternoon we are completely becalmed. Big drizzly clouds lumber alongside us and one drifts directly overhead, paints the deck dark brown, and abandons us to weak sunlight again. Everyone quiet and hypnotised. Towards dusk, Stewart tells me he once sailed up from Corunna through these waters in a tanker that had just been overhauled. A hurricane overtook them, stripping all the new paint off their ship, mangling ladders, dropping them in such deep hollows they couldn't see the horizon. Nearby were some small French fishing boats 'just bobbing up and down like corks. I could see the old boys leaning on the rails with their arms folded, staring at us. Just bobbing up and down like corks.'

When supper is over, Paul calls us up on deck. A school of dolphins is overtaking us to port. They're too far away to see clearly, and we can't hear them, but they're still magical – the bodies pulled taut, the mute white splash as they dive, the sense of zest and delight. We whistle and bang the side of the ship to call them closer but they ignore us, leaping in and out of their own world, intent on their own pleasure.

At midnight a dappling sound against the side of my cabin wakes me. We're moving. Then at 3.50 there's a tremendous rattling and creaking and the wind leaps up – just as though someone has started an engine. The ship jumps forward in long even bounds, heaving me from side to side in my bunk at first, then pinning me against the wall as we begin to make real headway. There's some energetic pumping from the heads as the watch changes, and excitement running through all the silent bunks. I am filled with expectation – though expectation of what, I'm not sure. Movement for its own sake. Getting nearer to whatever the next thing might be.

Falling asleep at last, I dream about John Clare. He's in the Asylum at High Beech in Essex, where the patients worked in the fields during the day, dressed in formal clothes. Clare never met Keats, though they shared a publisher. Clare referred to Keats as 'brother'.

It's a late summer field
of gleaners in line
backs bowed heads down
to glittering stubble

each of them dressed
in Victorian stuff
tail coats stiff collars
so maybe they're waiters

no that would be madness
these people are patients
just look over there
the lee of the haycart

that man is a doctor
he runs the asylum
where if you're not screaming
or stripping your clothes off

or searching the globe
for a fragment of nothing
you truss up your self
and bend to your duty

1 October. The wind veers slowly round to north-east, and the
Maria Crowther *gradually loses sight of land. As the cliffs of Dorset*
fade, Severn finds Keats on deck, poring over the sonnet 'Bright
Star'. Mistakenly, he thinks Keats has just written it; in fact he had
composed it several months before, and has now only transcribed it
to contemplate. 'Pillowed upon my fair love's ripening breast . . . So
live for ever – or else swoon to death.'

Sleep from 6 to 8, then on deck. A battlefield. Everything
drenched, the watch in padded boiler-suits and hats with flaps
over their ears. Rain clouds massing on all sides, with hot
sunshine squirting in between. After an hour or so, a squall
catches us – the bowsprit daggering into deep waves as we drive
ahead. We winch the bowsprit in a little – there's some danger it
might snap. As we do this, a tremendous wave leaps over the
bows, saturating us all and knocking Claire off her feet. She
slithers across the deck like someone riding down a snow-hill
on a tray, and crashes into the side. She's all right. Another huge

wave, this one filling our mouths, ears, pockets. We reel back to the stern like drunks returning from a party, and take shelter behind a flap of canvas by the tiller. But the rain still finds us, stinging, making us shout when we speak at all. Stewart says the crew think he should take in the topsail – it puts so much weight on the mast. But there's no need, he thinks. 'It's a good stick.' I squint up at its top. The weathervane looks jammed, it's so steady.

After three-quarters of an hour it's all over. The rain goes, and there's a moment of calm. The ship flops sickeningly. A gaggle of seagulls performs a flypast.

I scramble down to the chart room. By the end of yesterday we were 60 miles off the Spanish coast – too far east. With last night's and today's wind we are sailing north-west – going backwards, in fact, so we can get clear of Cape Finisterre.

Come mid-day, we've travelled far enough, and turn south again. Stewart thinks we should make Gibraltar within a week. Instinctively, I want to ask him what day we'll arrive, then realise it doesn't matter. I don't care. We must be coming near to the middle of May now, but that doesn't matter either.

They were the gods and you are only men;
go back to thinking how you might begin.

By mid-afternoon we're as far south as we were this time yesterday – but 40 miles further west. More sodden clouds surround us, but these look angrier than any we've seen before, and by evening the wind is strong. A storm is coming. After days of praying for wind, the thing itself is daunting. Skies going black, rigging beginning to whine, everyone shrugging into oilskins, tying ropes round their waists to lash themselves onto the ship. I glance along the deck and wonder whether I should be frightened.

It reaches us at sunset – gigantic swell, waves the size of houses, their tops whipped into foam and spuming over the bows. The bowsprit lunges into the water, vanishing altogether, then slicing up through collapsing white. The decks flood and empty, flood and empty, but the sea never gives up. It wants to smother us completely, charging towards us from all sides with a malicious indifference. It never occurs to me that we might sink. In fact it makes me want more – more rage, more danger. I want to dare it to turn me inside out, and at one point, when no one is looking, I untie myself from the rigging and move towards the bow, fastening myself on again where the waves will break over me more easily, drenching me.

I cling there for a hour, scoured and battered, then suddenly can't deal with it any more. A mixture of impatience and satiety. So I crawl down to my cabin, strip off my oilskins and stretch out. But there's no chance of sleep. Sleep isn't what I want. I want something definite and final. What I get is a whole new orchestra of creaks and moans – and something rapping against the cabin wall with sharp irregular clunks. I wedge a pillow against the wall by my head, another by my hips, and the angle of our sailing keeps me pressed there.

Around midnight, there's a burst of shouting. Perhaps this is what I'm waiting for. Perhaps this is it.

It is. Even in the darkness, I can feel the ship poised on the crest of a mountainous wave – then nothing. Just a wind-filled silence. We've taken off! We're flying! The whole length of the ship has launched clear of the sea and is ploughing through thin air. Only one thing can happen next, and I shut my eyes tight. Two. Three. Four. There's a shattering crash and roll, and a human groan runs through the entire length of the hull. It's a sound of exhaustion and supplication, but it won't do any good. The same thing is going to happen again. We take off, we lurch through space, we plummet down into a trough. I press my pillow over my head, as if I'm trying to suffocate myself, and can't tell how long I hold it there.

When I lift it away I can hear shouting again – but more orderly now – and the grind of the capstan winding in a sail. The water beside me is making its two sounds, the close-up gurgle and the further roaring rush. I get up and duck into the galley without knowing why. Liz is there, leaning against the table, staring at a crossword torn from a two-week-old paper. The table bucks and slides beneath our hands as we stumble through a few clues together. Current monthly account: 11 letters. Electricity bill. Water leaks onto our heads through the deck. Sticky brown water, stained with pitch.

2 October. *Favourable winds. The* Maria Crowther *is now out of sight of land, driving steadily south.*

Early next morning. The corridor outside my cabin is flooded – water rocking fiercely over a bundle of sail that's been flung down in the night. I squint up through the hatch. Heavy rain is driving in but I climb a few steps. The sky is thunderous, and enormous iron waves are crashing over the prow. Saturation. It's impossible to make myself heard, so I just stand there, my head poking out, listening to the kettle in the galley below me, slopping its water onto the hot-plate with a soothing *sssh, sssh, sssh*.

But I don't want to miss anything, which means I must duck back to my cabin, climb into my oilskins, then scuttle aft and tie myself back onto the rigging. The gale has blown all night – mostly force 9, now falling to 8. A container ship is smashing north, close to us, and Paul is hoisting the ensign. Water parted from the sea, as Keats said in his storm.

For the next hour we cling, or are pinned, to wherever we attached ourselves when first we came on deck. Someone is being sick in the bow, gripping the ropes as if crucified. Stewart, at the tiller, decides there's too much sail up, and gives orders I can barely hear. The crew tangling with the blocks and tackle on deck repeatedly vanish as walls of water shatter over them. Paul, in bare feet, climbs into a fold of the mainsail, threading a rope to reef it, and swings there like a child in a papoose. As the mast dips it takes him out over the sea, then hoists him upright again. He keeps shouting to Stewart. He's loving it.

At 10 the skies abruptly turn blue and the gale blows itself out. Nobody says anything. Nobody seems to know what to think. Is that all? Will it come back? For the next two hours we bowl along rapidly, the shadow of our sails casting over and away, the sunlight shielded, then released. Most of us barely slept last night, but we all stay on deck. The scrubbed sea. The bow-wave creaming. Clinton ties the tiller into position and sits on the rope as though it were a hammock. He knows the storm's over and has decided to be cheerful. 'Did you see Paul up there?' he asks, swinging his legs. 'Think of all those poor buggers at home now, in their offices. Brrrr!'

Around lunch time another smaller school of dolphins sweeps close to the boat on the port side. But they show no interest in us and silently disappear. On the stern, at exactly the same time, an empty yellow life jacket. 'Nobody in it,' says Stewart quietly. The rest of the crew look away. A little later, we hear an urgent voice bursting onto the radio – a boat calling Finisterre. 'Charley Alpha Foxtrot. Charley Alpha Foxtrot'. Finisterre answers. 'Medico, medico,' says the voice, but we can't hear why. The voice breaks up and there's nothing else.

At 7, the sea and sky steadier, a big wind still following. Fifteen or twenty more dolphins bomb towards us through the swell. Pale wriggling bellies and sleek backs just visible inside their cliff of water, then leaping and diving as they reach the trough. They shoal round the prow, slinking over and under each other, up to and away from the ship, making excited high-pitched whinnies. Each one appeals to us by seeming intimate, here for our sake: the candid roll to show their neutral undersides; the shaved cunt of their blowholes as they break the surface; their mouths carved in a cartoon smile. But of course they are pleasing themselves, not us. We mean nothing to them, and when they have played long enough they simply shear away. We go down to supper in silence.

Before bed we hang the topsail, unreef the mainsail and mizzen. With eight of us, it takes an hour of hard work. In the old days, there used to be a crew of five. The ship settles easily when this is done – the seas subsiding and sweeping us forward. In the last 24 hours we've made 130 miles – more than twice what we managed in Biscay.

*

The wind sat in the north-east all night and now there's a spectacular dawn – the sun straining and blobbing in purple clouds, then hesitating, hesitating, before erupting into triumphant blue.

At 9, when it's already warm, there's a weather report of a gale in south Finisterre. Paul's heard it, and we question him in succession, each wanting him to say something new. Will there be any wind for us? Will we get where we want to be? He tells us everything will be all right, but we don't believe him. Anyway, we're hardly in Finisterre now. We're in Trafalgar.

Trafalgar. On land, history leaves its scar however we plough up battlefields, tear down buildings, spread new estates and factories. Out here it leaves no mark; it just survives in the names. The Solent, where people watched the Spanish Armada blow past, then waited for Napoleon, and Hitler. Corunna, which we passed the day before yesterday. Cape St Vincent and Trafalgar which are to come. Their names roll through my head and I see ripped sails, cracked masts, blazing rigging – but none of it for long. In a moment I'm watching the waves again. The one to come like the one gone by. Always new but always the same.

By mid-day there's no wind at all – just low, flat, grey, unbroken cloud.

Something inside me gives way. I slump at my place in the stern all afternoon, watching the wind run its hand listlessly down the sails, boredom overwhelming me. This is not boredom like before – not a trance. This is real nothing. Nothing which gouges a hole in my skull and drags out my eyes on stalks to stare into it: failure; despair; disgust curdling into rage. When one of the crew comes up to me I look straight through him. Then he belches vilely and grins: 'Wind.' I want to stick a marlin spike up his arse and throw him to the shark which has just idled past, its fin slick and alert.

No change at 6.30, when a face looks out of a hatch and calls 'Supper'. It's the last thing I want. I just want today done with and over. 'Come on. Supper.' I force myself down into the galley. Each plate is piled enormously. The stove puffs and simmers in its corner.

Then back to the stern again, watching our wake form and scribble itself out, form and scribble itself out. An almost unlivable day. At home, days can be steered round, or drunk into oblivion. This one has just had to be endured. Two hours until it's worth even trying to sleep, and the prospect of the same thing tomorrow. Please God make the wind blow.

15 October. The Maria Crowther *is caught in a severe storm as she reaches the Bay of Biscay. The passengers are all ill and take to their bunks once again.*

My dream last night. It was the past. I had bought a house by the sea with a woman called Anna, who I don't know in real life, and everywhere was furnished in a fussy, baroque style (the light bulbs were shaped like tulip heads, and not all of them worked). It was evening – a fierce, flickering, electric sunset – and I was showing the house to Anna's two brothers. Through their eyes, some rooms looked strange and gorgeous, others mad and shabby. One brother was surprised by our lack of books, and I told him we kept them in two rooms apart, neither of which he'd seen yet. In the sitting-room, which overlooked the green-weedy shore and menacing sea, I pointed out a little summer house at the end of a promontory, beyond the garden. He said the whole house was worth buying just for that – its solitude. Then I went to bed, alone.

I was woken – still in my dream – by the sound of frantic pumping and calls for help. I went to see what the matter was, and found the other brother struggling to keep the lavatory door shut. When he opened it a crack, floods of shitty black water poured out, slopping round our ankles. I left him to it and went into the garden. It was still evening. Still the same fitful, threatening light.

Anna was playing croquet, muffing a shot as I came up to her and furious. I felt that I had gone to bed too early – that I'd offended her, since there was obviously some kind of party going on, and she had expected me to be there. As we stood beside each other, one of the guests half-traipsed, half-danced past me – a hideous big-boned woman wearing a blood-coloured chiffon dress which fluttered in the sea-wind. She had boils on her face and thick, muscular, bulging shaved legs. I wanted to talk but my tongue wouldn't work. 'Stop mumbling,' Anna said, seething. I tried to say: 'This means one of three things. Either you love someone else. Or you want to leave me. Or . . .' I couldn't remember the third thing. I felt utterly powerless, wretched, at a loss. And I woke up.

For a while I lay in the darkness. I thought: no one else will see why, but this is the worst dream I have ever had. Ever. My heart was pounding, legs rigidly crossed at the ankles, hands folded over my chest and stuffed into my armpits.

Collecting myself, I heard something slinking against my cabin wall. Something I knew perfectly well, but which after a day's silence already seemed strange. Water, of course. Water purling past me. We were moving again: the tackle clunking in its iron horse as we changed course; the boom giving its tiny squeak as the mainsail filled.

I angled myself across the bunk so that I matched the angle of the ship. As the slow hours rippled past, their minutes broke into half-minutes, their half-minutes into seconds. And as each fragment snapped off and fell away a wave broke in its wake. Not a wave fribbling against the hull, but a wave inside my head. I was being cleaned out. I was being rubbed away. When I fell asleep towards dawn, I had diluted into the nothing around me. It was what I wanted. I felt released.

But climbing on deck at 8 – a row of glum faces. The wind has shifted to the south and all night we've sailed due east, making no progress down our course.

I stand next to Stewart at the tiller, expecting this new disappointment to crash down on me, squaring my shoulders to take its load. But whatever happened last night is still working. It doesn't matter any more that we can't meet deadlines. I couldn't care less that our schedule is wrecked. What matters is being here – seeing these things I'll never see again, feeling the things I shall never feel to such depth.

The mood elsewhere on the ship is very low. Liz has pinned up a notice in the galley saying our water is running out – now we can only use so much a day. And the one head which has coped with the pissings, crappings and vomitings of six people for the last two weeks is finally packing in. After breakfast I pump it clear, but it fills remorselessly with yellow-brown water.

Paul organises a deck-scrub – more to rally people than to meet a need – and as I duck forward to collect my long-handled broom, I look directly ahead. There's misty drizzle, and a tight yellow amphitheatre of sun in which I see something I don't immediately recognise.

Land.

A ridge of hills, a stratum of pink and white houses. The sun fades immediately and the scene with it, but inside half an hour the whole coast is back again. A town straight ahead, docks to the left.

We crowd into the bows, clumped together like people in a photograph. This should be marvellous, I tell myself, and hold my breath waiting for it to strike. But nothing happens. Not like the other kinds of nothing I have known before – this time it's just emptiness. The docks grow clearer – the insect-cranes and the ziggurat-containers. And the shore – a bow of white sand, and a fairground just beyond the ridge of dunes. There's a big top, the sloping roof striped pink and cream. The Ferris wheel hangs at a standstill. The beach is deserted.

'What do you think was the first thing Mrs da Gama said to Vasco when he came back?' I ask no one in particular.

'Christ, you smell,' says Stewart. 'That's what my wife always says to me.'

Everyone laughs, but it's thin, melancholy laughter. I turn away down the deck. I don't want to see this place. It's too soon. I'm not ready. I haven't finished thinking whatever it is I'm thinking. And I don't want to leave the ship either. Not this ship and not these people.

'What land is it?' I hear somebody asking.

'Oporto,' comes the answer.

'Foreign land,' says Stewart.

That's right. Foreign land.

16 October. Today, and for the next two weeks, the Maria
Crowther *sails steadily south, stalling briefly in a calm off Cape St
Vincent, at the southern tip of Portugal, and hoving to shortly after-
wards when they are challenged by a man-o'-war. Keats's health
improves as he approaches Gibraltar, but when he enters the
Mediterranean he haemorrhages badly, and the last week before they
reach Naples is hard going.*

Yesterday there was a decision to take. We need water and
provisions. Should we have put in at Oporto, or headed on
south for Lisbon, 100 miles away? It seemed best to keep going,
which meant Lisbon.

All last afternoon, and all night, we tacked along the
Portuguese coast. Around dawn, there is the dismal clank of the
anchor going down. We've stopped. For what feels like the
millionth time, I squeeze out of the hatch on deck and squinny
round. We're off a bare beach – a beach identical to the one we
saw yesterday, only now there's a black jetty away to the right,
and different dock cranes faintly visible beyond it.

Stewart calls us round the tiller. He tells us we've only made
40 miles since Oporto and this means Lisbon is impossible – we
need the provisions too badly. We have to turn back. 'How can
we do that?' someone asks, and we all stare at the sky as if we
didn't know what was there. Emptiness is there. Clouds like the
smoke from wet sticks. The reflection of charcoal waves. We
are completely becalmed.

The crew drift away, avoiding each other's eyes.

That accident in heaven over there –
those slintered spars and timbers smashed to bits
where God slipped up and almost broke in two
the sky-door of his attic but still clings to it –

that must mean storms for someone. Not for us.
We're in the weather hollow: snaffling wind,
the sun scarfed-up, warm drizzle, and the sea
revolving in its sleep time out of mind.

To think it brought us signs and wonders once!
(A once long gone, a once so far away
we might have made it up.) It brought us dolphins
schooled and surfing down sloped walls of spray;

it brought a whale, a sleek black submarine
which groaned, which fired its fountain-head,
and sank; it brought us starlight inside waves;
it brought; it brought; it brought. But like I said,

all this in time we might have never lived –
all this and something else: the five-foot shark
we hooked and hauled on deck. Its bitter eyes
were hatred pooled in slits of oily dark.

Its metal skin would rasp our own skin raw.
Its mouth, lopsided where the barb dragged through
and senile with despair, was death itself.
I took a photograph. You see? I told you so.

As heat concentrates over the land, a feeble wind gathers, and
by early afternoon we have started to tack north up the coast
again. I doze in the lifeboat, clasping my hands behind my head.
The sun comes out, the long beach unwinds, the hills gather and
step out of their mist. That's our destination ahead – where
those chimneys are billowing – but we never seem to get any
closer. I curl down into my nest. I could stay like this for ever,
living this in-between life.

*

It seems years since someone said: you never know what's going to happen next at sea. We expected to drift back along the coast, no trouble, but a strong south-westerly arrived in the early hours, and by dawn we're churning off Oporto in North Sea weather. There's cold, driving rain. The clouds are so low they even cover the tops of cranes in the port.

At 10, Stewart gets word that he can enter the harbour. Has he let them know we don't have an engine? He once told me, a long time ago, that ships like *Excelsior* never sink – they only go down when they hit something. And this is a difficult entrance: a narrow dog's leg. A gigantic grey stone pier to the left, a snub smaller one to the right, and the strong cross wind.

The crew stand at their stations by the rigging, waiting for orders, but Stewart keeps his eyes on the two piers. Then he angles the ship as if she were a dart, one massive hand gripping the throat of the tiller.

'Everybody ready? Here we go.'

It's finished almost before it starts, leaving me no time to feel anything. We whisk over the struggling waves, the sheltering walls loom round us, and the crew collapse the sails in a crashing flurry, both booms thumping down like wreckage. 'Drop the hook!' Stewart shouts. 'Drop it now!' The anchor chain makes its scrabbling rush and we stop dead, the ship groaning as we slew round to starboard. Paul cheers, standing among the heaped-up sails like someone who's killed a dragon. 'You won't often see sailing like that', he says, grinning at me. Bill shouts 'Tobacco!'

Everything immediately slows down. The water lies in a calm sweat. We all stand motionless – self-conscious, as if we were learning how to live in a different climate: how to behave and how to survive.

The first thing is simply to look around.

It's a dismal place. Through the rain: an abstract of orange and white containers; a tanker with a lop-sided lifeboat dangling astern; the cement wall of the harbour daubed with the names of absent ships; fishing boats trailing clouds of seagulls.

A giant digger is filling a Russian tanker with gravel; every few minutes there's a battering roar as another load tips in.

For the first time since leaving London, I feel sick. If we're going to get off here, I want to do it immediately. I want to mark the change and begin to understand it. But we need a tug to get us to shore – without our engine, we're stranded.

A life-size plastic arm, torn from a doll, twists past us. The fingers have hooked a tuft of black weed.

I remember that I should have been able to smell the land when we first saw it yesterday; in fact I smelt nothing. But there's something now, all right: the stench of sewage rolling over and over us in a mouldy wave.

After five hours, an enormous tug throbs alongside and throws two ropes astern, one big orange tie at the front. It's like watching TV – vivid but nothing to do with me. The trim-looking man at the helm with his tartan shirt and metal-frame specs: he looks like a bank clerk. The brutal rearing prow with 'Monte Xisto' in big white letters.

But something goes wrong. The tug's too powerful to tow us safely, and as the thick orange fore-rope takes the strain it wrenches the stanchion away from *Excelsior*'s hull. A cruel splintering crack travels across deck, and one of the crew gives a scream, as though they've seen a person injured. After all we've done, all the bludgeonings and becalmings, it's a machine which hurts us.

I don't want to see any more, and go down to my cabin. When everything's quiet again, when I've heard us thump against the harbour wall, I come back on deck and head straight for the ladder ashore. This moment should be extraordinary, I know that, but all I want to do is get it over with.

Each rung of the ladder is covered with sewage-stinking mud. It's revolting but I keep going, not caring, and claw forwards for a few yards on my hands and knees when I reach the top. Then I stand foolishly, trying to wipe the wet goo off one hand with my other wet hand, and begin staggering as the ground heaves beneath me.

I'm in a timber yard. Whole, colossal tree trunks are stacked ahead of me, yellow numbers scrawled on their bark, and a bulldozer is lumbering towards them like a dinosaur going into battle. I step backwards and lose my footing in the pulpy mud. I don't understand. Surely I shouldn't be here? It's not safe. I scuttle back down the ladder again and onto the boat.

Stewart is running his hand over the stanchion, where the tug wrecked it. 'It'll mend.' He walks to the stern with his head down and I follow. What we have to say is so obvious, neither of us wants to start talking. We just sit there side by side, the harbour wall steaming and reeking beside us. When I look back, there's only a patch of scummy black water, washing against breeze blocks. A dead puppy is wedged there, fawn belly bloated, stiff legs skyward.

I climb the iron ladder again, the earth still wobbly, and set off across the timber yard, looking for a bar.

*

Early next morning the provisions arrive. Then another tug, a smaller one, blathers towards us and by 9 we're in open sea again. There's a steady wind from the north, polishing and clearing the sky. The long white curve of the shore is flung out beside us, straight and simple as an arm on a bed. Bill is standing by the broken stanchion, scraping mud off the rail.

I know what he's thinking – what all the crew are thinking. It doesn't matter any more how late we are. It doesn't matter how many storms have shaken us and how many calms marooned us: we have suffered all these things and survived. We have paid the price for our journey.

I settle into the stern, where I have sat for 1,000 miles, and stare straight ahead. Everything will be all right now. In a week we shall be passing Gibraltar – Keats said it glowed in the water 'like a topaz'. Then, in another week, Naples. The wind presses evenly against my back and the waves in front of us open and close like a million eyes blinking. Yes, everything will be all right now. I have seen what there is to see; the journey is already beginning to end.

I look into our wake once more, putting my hand to my eyes. There is Keats, signalling to me from 200 years away. He is writing something down, throwing it forward for me to catch, and I will read it. Now he is speaking – I can see his wide mouth moving. But the wind and waves drown what he says; his voice never reaches me. I guess. I imagine. I suppose. Possibly. Probably. Perhaps. The breeze shifts but we still creak forwards, leaving him further and further behind. Doing our best and hoping.

2

Naples harbour. Naples. I wait for the exhilaration to strike me, but all that comes is a kind of creeping carefulness. I am bothered by what date it is, and can't decide. Late May. That will have to do.

We are sailing slowly into the dead centre of the bay; there's moist, mid-afternoon sunlight and listless air. Sloppy waves. After the open sea, the water here seems to have no depth or secret life. Yet there's a fishing boat by the harbour wall, and two men feeding a golden net off the stern. They must be expecting something. And there are boys on top of the harbour wall, too, flicking out lines with long rods.

An argument is yammering in the back of my head. One voice tells me that everything I've seen at sea matters more than anything I'll see on land. The other voice says the land-world is the real world – I must find my happiness there or not at all. I feel detached from them both, letting the argument roll on.

But this is Naples, I tell myself again; this is where you wanted to be. Look at it!

I stretch my eyes wide. To my left, the jam-packed harbour of Santa Lucia. Straight ahead, the Castel del Angelo – a squat honey-coloured giant on its promontory. The *Maria Crowther* would have moored just here, in that same shadow. I stare at the cannon-scarred walls, willing something to come clear. To my right, Vesuvius above the suburbs. The slate-thin cloud, tilting on the summit, dissolves as I watch. There's the ruined mouth of the crater, dipping on one side and brimming with black mist.

I look and look, but still feel nothing. My eyes fidget and swivel away to the green smudge of coast slicing down past Pompeii to Sorrento. All out of sight.

This sleepiness I feel – it's a sort of evasion. All my irritation, all the frustration and anger, have evaporated. On this deck, in this little space, I've held myself steady and undistracted. I've peered down through the lid of my skull and seen myself swimming in the clear water of each minute.

21 October. The Maria Crowther *reaches Naples but is detained in quarantine for ten days. Keats is exhausted and ill; he writes to Charles Brown telling him that during this time 'My health suffered more from bad air and a stifled cabin then it had done the whole voyage.'*

For the first time in weeks, a day split into differences.

In the morning, to Pompeii; then back to Naples, to the

Guanti Nuovi district, where Keats stayed for a few days before travelling to Rome – his house was destroyed when the area was developed in the '60s. A gaggle of children watch me watching, soon bored but thinking they'll miss something as soon as they go. And a crowd of adults, gathered outside a vegetable shop. A melon-faced fellow who carries crutches and sits on a crate. A sleek younger man – his son? He looks like an aubergine. Another: a warty lemon. A woman with hair like a dead lettuce. Her friend has a vest like a string bag. They're a complete set in Happy Families. The Fruit-and-Vegetable Family.

Doodling through the narrow, steeply climbing streets, I have to nip on and off the pavement as mopeds rev behind me, ducking to miss awnings and washing.

Back to the bay in the afternoon, then the cloisters of San Girolomini. By now there's a strong sun carving shadows on the walls, splintering through the glossy leaves of lemon and orange trees. Half a dozen moggies follow me, keeping to the shade. One gives a wheezing hiccup with every breath and clenches its eyes shut in pain. Everything else feels padded, protected.

At dusk, a taxi to Posillipo, high up, where couples come to gaze out over the city and kiss. I squeeze between them to the rail. The sunlight has gone purple. The volcano is sleeping in its mist-shroud.

The world is a brilliantly constructed fake – I can't connect with anything in it. The miraculous ingenuity of buildings! The genius and daring of traffic! My eye pans wherever it wants to go, irresponsible. I skim above the ships in the harbour, the people congregating and wandering, putting their heads down and hurrying.

And further off – the other, dead city at Pompeii. I didn't feel so this morning, but now its shadow-vaulted rooms, its lost ceilings and wheel-scarred streets – now all these seem more actual than the living city beside it.

24 October. Keats writes to Fanny's mother in Hampstead: 'If I were well enough there is enough in this Port of Naples to fill a quire of paper – but it looks like a dream – every man who can row his boat and walk and talk seems a different being from myself – I do not feel in the world . . . O what an account I could give you of the Bay of Naples if I could once more feel myself a Citizen of this world.'

What did it mean to say goodbye to the ship? To a *thing*? I walked slowly from prow to stern, studying the rigging, the deckboards, the blocks, the capstan as though I'd never seen them before. The ropes with their blackened sections where the crew wiped their hands clean. The hatches and their pale brown paint scored with brush-marks. The blocks worn smooth and gleaming. I want to remember these things for ever. They are the signs that my life need not always be the one I am living.

The crew stood in an awkward circle and we shook hands. When I reached Stewart we both took a step forward as though about to embrace, then changed our minds. He was wearing his orange 'Port of Felixstowe' jacket. How exhausted he looked! We banged each other on the arm – bouf – and turned apart. A moment later, from the far side of the harbour, I looked back and saw him hesitating on deck. If I had called out he would have heard me, but I didn't know what to say. I stretched both arms above my head and waved for a long time. He did the same.

And now the ship has already started to fade, to lose its separateness and confuse with other things. This morning, for instance, in the Via Pallonetto S Lucia. A stepped street climbing under an arch of washing. Transistors competing on the high balconies and someone letting down a green bowl with keys in it. Someone else throwing a broom at a dog.

This afternoon in the Piazza Plebiscito and the San Carlo theatre, which Keats visited. My eyes still slide off everything I see – the statues with their chipped noses, the high stucco walls, the pompous façades and blazing interiors. And my brain won't admit the things people say. Sophia Loren was born near here; Oscar Wilde drank in this café; Ferdinand IV had a son known as 'The Bomb'; this is the plant used to make Christ's crown of thorns. I touched the sharky stem and deliberately prick myself. It doesn't hurt at all.

*

We take the road to Rome – the same Keats took – and stop at Solfatara.

I've heard about this place. It's a kind of offshoot from Vesuvius – a sulphur field where they used to bring tubercular patients to breathe the stinking air and wallow in the sauna heat. It's supposed to look like Hell – though in the old days, they reckoned the Elysian Fields were hereabouts, somewhere under these half-built houses and tatty hotels. The entrance to the Underworld was further off, nearer the volcano.

I pitch into the sun and stop short. Across a wide white disc of dry sulphur, the ground rises into a hill of steaming earth. Not just steaming, either. Actually smoking and bubbling, firing off steady jets of smoke, glopping and gurgling and shifting. I am shown through into a fenced-off section, following carefully in the steps of a gigantic black-bearded custodian. Vulcan. He shows me where I can walk safely, and where I will fall through.

I stand still and think about this. He's telling me: if I step off this path, I'll sink through the surface of the earth. I'm wearing thick shoes, but the heat comes through all the same, and the stench of sulphur makes me dizzy.

I look down and suppose I'm about to imagine myself disappearing. In fact what I see is myself emerging. Head and shoulders bursting up through the red-hot crust, lava flaking off me like water. Then the rest of me comes clear, hands at my sides, straight as a missile, rising back onto the surface of the world.

All afternoon, we drive north to Rome – past Monte Casino and Sperlonga, through Terracina where Keats stayed, following the route of the Appian Way. In Terracina a fragment of the old road survives – ragged hunks of stone, desperately uneven. No wonder Severn walked most of the way, throwing flowers into the carriage where Keats lay exhausted.

Their journey took a week; we reach Rome by 8. Twice, maybe more, we pass prostitutes standing at the roadside. They spin on high heels, sheltering their eyes from the grit-wake we leave behind us. In the gaps between factories and villages, beyond advertisement hoardings and eucalyptus groves, the country flicks past in pieces: rush-clumps wagging along canals; a field of buffalo; a glimpse of coastline with its volcano-rubble. At one point a flying-boat lumbers alongside us, then curves out to sea.

I sit in the front of the bus drinking beer and thinking about my mother – everything about her: her accident, the hospitals, her death. It takes more than two hours, and I am burying her as we reach the outskirts, my heart lifting at the wide streets and pine trees in the sinking sun.

I am coming back to life.

15 November – 23 February 1821. Keats and Severn lodge in a house at the foot of the Spanish Steps. To start with, Keats is able to walk a little, and there are still hopes for his recovery. For the last six weeks of his life he is bed-bound, haemorrhaging badly, longing for death. 'Did you ever see anyone die?' he asks Severn at one point. 'Well then, I pity you.' Severn cooks for him, comforts him, nurses him. When the end finally approaches, Keats calls out to him 'Severn – Severn – lift me up for I am dying – I shall die easy – don't be frightened – thank God it has come.'

To Keats's house. After his death, all his furniture and movables were destroyed – as Italian law demanded. Later still, most of the rooms were altered, too. But his bedroom is the same: the room where he died.

It's early morning, and I climb towards him through a warm near-silence. The room is so small! Like a cabin, only taller. And the water crashing outside is so loud! I peer through the window. There is the fountain in the square below – a sinking ship; the pale blue waves, jagged with reflections, skittering over the broken mast and sides. Wreckage and violent death. The end of the journey.

Here was his bed, along this right-hand wall; this was the glass he leant against, sickening, then lay down and looked through. The ceiling is the same, too – row after row after row of wide-eyed daisies. 'I can feel the daisies growing over me,' he told Severn. I stretch out on the floor and examine them, the coldness of the tiles seeping through my shirt and under my skin.

Then I kneel at the fireplace. This is what he must have seen, day after day, huddled in his bed. It's low and narrow – plain grey stone except for a frieze above the grate which shows two grimacing heads. The same head, larger, is in the centre. I bend closer. It's not a head but a face – a devil's face – tongue stuck out hard, eyes stretching wide with anger and disgust.

Behind my back, Keats is emaciated and wretched. The light swells and fades as his days pass. The fountain throws its water-shadows across the ceiling. Voices rise and fall. The little cabin-room holds still for a while, then begins to shift forwards and slip-slide. Dissolving.

Here is his death-mask in a display cabinet. The life mask beside it is fleshed-out and eager, the wide top lip jutting slightly over the lower, even under the weight of plaster. The death-mask is smaller – shrunken. Nose beaky. Cheeks hollow. Hair brushed back so I can see how much had fallen out. Just a thin stripe in the centre of his forehead. It is not an exhausted face but an empty one. A drained-out face, scooped and flayed.

The devil is still poking out his tongue. Water in the fountain is battering over the sides of the drowned ship.

26 February. Doctors perform an autopsy on Keats and discover that his lungs are almost completely destroyed. They are surprised that he has lived so long. He was twenty-five years old. Next day he is buried – outside the city walls and in darkness, as the Roman law required.

The Protestant Cemetery. I've been here before, and know where to find him. There's soft, clear sunlight and no wind. I am becalmed.

The bell clanks, the door in the gateway opens, and I turn left through the first, jumbled part of the graveyard into the more spacious section where he lies. It's in the far corner, beyond those pine trees, where someone is taking flowers out of a twist of paper and spreading them on the ground.

I keep walking. The pyramid of Cestius holds up its sightless triangular mirror. A heavy pine-cone unhinges and crashes to earth; there is an explosion of yellow sap. Cats appear everywhere, prowling through the strawberry-woven grass, slinking round the tombs.

The man leaving flowers vanishes and I keep walking. But I'm not getting anywhere. I can't compete with the backwards-rolling earth. It lifts me through the room where he died, past the sinking-ship fountain, over the jagged stones at Terracina, above the warren of Naples, and out into the bay.

I come to a standstill on deck, in the middle of nowhere, one hand holding the rigging, the other shading my face. There's no land, no gulls, no fish rising, nothing. Just the big greasy waves slithering forward, the thump and squelch of water against the prow. I remember that I have been more bored here than I thought possible. I have been half out of my mind. I have thought that I stood in the ante-chamber to death itself. Now I can't feel any of these things. Now I am only and exactly where I want to be, wind and sunlight swarming all over me, riding the roll and rise of pure pleasure.

Come back, is all I want to say. Come back and let me have it again. This time I will know what it means to feel happy.

Then I am standing behind him, resting both hands on the warm stone.

The man who was laying flowers on the grave has re-appeared. He has a wide-mouthed face and swept-back brown hair. I look straight into his eyes and start talking.